MOTHER'S DAY

KATE CAVANAUGH

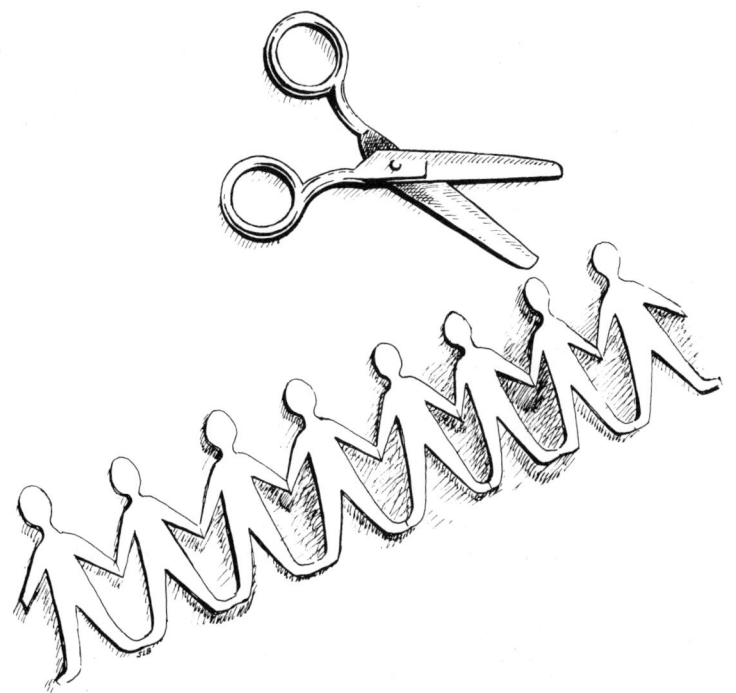

MOTHER'S DAY

KAC Inc.
Omaha, Nebraska
1989

Copyright © 1989 by Kate Cavanaugh

All rights reserved. Except as permitted under the Copyright Act of 1976, no part of this book may be reproduced or distributed in any form or by any means or stored in a data base retrieval system, without the prior written permission of the author.

Printed in the United States of America
by Cockle Printing Company
Omaha, Nebraska

Library of Congress No. 89-083480
ISBN 0-9622353-0-X
First printing April, 1989

Cartoons by Jim Horan and Dave Croy.
Reprinted with permission of
Jim Horan, Dave Croy and *Omaha World Herald*.

Columns from March, 1977 to September, 1983
originally published by Sun Newspapers of Omaha, Inc.

Columns from April, 1985 to January, 1989
originally published by *Omaha World Herald*.

Cover design and cartoons for Chapters two and three
by Sandi Bruns.

Back cover photograph by John Cavanaugh.

To John: "You're in my heart, you're in my soul, you'll be my breathe should I grow old, you are my lover, you're my best friend, you're in my soul."

by Rod Stewart, Warner Bros. Records Inc.

Acknowledgements

I want to acknowledge and thank my family.

My parents, Bill and Evelyn Barrett, who taught me to love life.

My parents-in-law, the late Jack Cavanaugh and Kathleen Cavanaugh, who loves me like a daughter.

My husband, John, the love of my life.

My children: Patrick, Colleen, Maureen, Machaela, John, Michael, Peter, and Matthew, who fill my life with love.

The Barrett and Cavanaugh brothers, sisters and their families, whom I love so much.

John and Patt Barrett, Chris and Kathy Reller; Mike, Bonnie, Joey and Julie Butcher; Peter Barrett; Bill, Barbara, Megan, Joe, and Jim Plachinski; Mary Pat Barrett, Phil Teague, and Barrett Teague; Ken, Sheila, and Max Wippich; Bill Barrett; Jerry, Mary Anne, Jerry Jr. and Kathy Lucas; Mike, Cathie, Erin, Diane, Sarah, and John Amdor; Jim, Pat, Molly and Anne Cavanaugh; Tom and Bertille DeBaudiniere Cavanaugh; Steve, Margaret Mary, and Claire Boyer.

Putting this book together put me in touch with many people. Some I've known all my life and some I've met in the process. Each one contributed in an invaluable way.

Thank you: Jean Tobin, Louise Runyan, Tim Runyan, Kathy Rowen, Susan Harr, Brian Harr, Burke Harr, Lori Liekhus, Nancy Jorgensen, Karen Swartz, Larry Novicki, Woody Howe, Pat Waters, Adella Wacker, Cate Petersen, George Miller Jr., Harold Andersen, Susan Laughlin, Teena Beehner, Chris Sodoro, Chris Haschke, Colleen Campbell, Liz Empson, Sharon Krauss, Jim Clemon, Julie Hefflinger, Nikki Welch, Tom Welch, Cindi Finnigan, Ellen Finnigan, Harry Otis, Sandy Kelly, Nancy Hornstein, Jill Hornstein, Jim Horan, Cindy Cawley, Claudia Boehm, Sister Marian Camel, Sandi Bruns, Andy Cockle, Sherry Tallman, Dolores Vipond, Noany Dougherty, Dan Dougherty, Peter Hoagland, Jim Crounse, Paul Landow, Betsy Freeland, David Hosakawa, Tom Giitter, Molly Romero, Nancy Thompson, Janie Kolbeck, Jean Crouchley, John Green, Judy Schweikart, Michelle Sullivan, Andrea Randone, Jeanette Randone, Assist Business Services, Dave Croy, Mary Fogarty, Roderick Atwater, Teresa Bloomingdale, Joe Baversco, Bridget Diederich, Kerin Staup, Jennifer Bartak, Heather Hall, Melanie Carlson, Susan Bromm, Trish Barber, Dave Flynn, Diane Flynn, Mark McMillan, Peg Tentinger Buttner, Richard Cohen, Janet Davis, Tom Fogarty, Ivy Harper, Esther Vaughan, Pat Coonan, and my sixth and seventh grade English teacher, Sister Frances Gertrude O.P.

Contents

INTRODUCTION
Grandma Hardt Was Really Something   xiii

1 LET'S TALK ABOUT ME
Life's Little Headaches Are Put in Perspective   3
Rustling of Mice Makes a Strong Mother Feel Trapped Like a Rat   4
Sleepless Night Hits High Gear   6
Frantic Mom Dressed to Kill   9
Writing a Column is Better Than Being Ann Landers   11
Fashion is Nice, But a Good Bargain is Better   15
Gas Gauge Hovering on Empty, But Kate's Late   17
Lefties Elbowed in a Right-Handed World   19
'Wonder Years' for Teens, 'Worry Years' for Parents   21
'What Do I Owe You?' Is Not a Simple Question   23
Case of 'I Should Be's' Is a Daily Dilemma   25

2 NATIVITY SCENES
Machaela Cavanaugh Was Worth Waiting For   29
Hands: Independent, but Loving   31
Kate Has Another Man in Her Life   32
Two Sisters Share the Spoils of Maternity   34
She Never Expected To Be Expecting Again   35
Ritual of Motherhood Means Buying a New Nightgown   37
Family Makes Room for One More   39
Friends Greet New Baby, And Boy, Can They Cook   41
Happy St. Mother's Day   43

3 MARRIED TO A MEMBER, LIFE IN WASHINGTON DC
The Thrill of Washington Continues for Kate   49
Why does Jimmy Carter Envy Kate Cavanaugh?   50

    White House Picnic Makes Kate's Heart Pound   52
    The Campaign is Over – Oh, What a Relief It Is!   54
    Kate Enjoys Fairyland Evening at White House   56
    Could Kate's Kitchen Be The New Sans Souci?   58
    The Reason Why Women Work by Richard Cohen THE WASHINGTON POST   60
    Kate's Not Ready Yet To Be Age 35   63
    Kate Has An Evening of Enchantment   64
    Patrick Sums up Iran: 'A Big Mess'   66
    Kate Glances Back . . . and Looks Ahead   68
    People Make The Difference   70

4 BUMS LIVE HERE
    Questions Reveal Compulsion to Clean House   75
    Homes Hatch Plots to Spend Owner's Money   76
    Not Only Cans Collect Garbage   78
    Those Cereal Dishes Must Be 'Bulldozed'   80
    Kitchen Remodeling Cooks Up Chaos   82
    Bill System Delays Day of Reckoning   84
    From Tiny Samples, Big Decisions Grow   85
    Kids' Lazy Days of Summer Can Drive a Mother Crazy   87
    This Old Pan Is Chock-Full of Memories   89
    Do-It-Yourselfer Plumbs the Mysteries of Clogged Pipes   92
    Baskets Brim with the 'Stuff' That Homes Are Made Of   94

5 JUNK IS A FOOD GROUP
    Girl Scout Cookies Scattered Over House By Kids Taking a Bite Out of the Profits   99
    Who Are The Wise Guys Labeling Cereal 'Free inside'?   100
    No Fuss, No Mess Goals In Choosing Fast Foods   102
    Boxed Macaroni, Cheese Is Their Gourmet Delight   105
    Good Food Travels Fast   107
    Good Food or Just Good for You?   109

Plan to Serve 'Simple Meal' Proves To Be a
Contradiction in Terms   111

6 YOU'RE CUTE AND THAT'S WHAT'S IMPORTANT

Readying for Church Is Hardly a Religious Experience   115
Kate Plays Landlady to a Stuffed Menagerie   117
Reluctant Date, Mom Enjoy Prep's Prom   118
5-Year-Old's Eyes Can Make a Mom Forget Strait-Laced Shoe Budget   121
Giving Up TV Left More Time for Fighting   123
Can a Parent Ever Be Ready for Son's Driver's License Test?   125
Slow Service Steams the Customers at 'Cavanaugh Cafe'   127
Welcome to Patrick's Island   129
Wedding Bells Aren't Chiming in Boys' Plans for Life   131
New Phone Technology Has Familiar Ring   133
Milestones for Teens Part of Life's Canvas   136

7 MY POST GRADE SCHOOL DEGREE

Cranky Children: Some Mornings, Only a Family Could Love Them   141
Kids' School Routine Is Never That for Mom   142
She Needn't Have Studied . . . Homework Helper Repeating Grades   144
Dash for Picnic Supplies Cost $48.63   146
Mom Finished Her Homework in the Eighth Grade   148

8 HOOPLA AND HAPPY TIMES

All-Nighters Sleep Where They Fall   153
Birthday Season Is a Happy Time of Hoopla   155
Birthday Luau at 'Waikiki Basement' Is Another Event That Got Out of Hand   157
Party a Great Excuse for Grand Illusions   159
Job of Eating Leftovers Falls to the Party Hostess   161
Saying 'I do' Is the Easy Part   163
Democracy's Birthday Deserves All the Hoopla   165

Able-Bodied Dancers Toss the Salad, Shake Their
    Tail Feathers   166
She Must Be a Saint to Organize a Haunted House   168
Over the River and Through the Years   171
Joy to the World! Family Photo Passes Muster for
    Christmas Card   173
Magic Sets Today Apart from Rest of the Year   175

9 BELL BOTTOMS WILL BE BACK
Tons of Sisters, and Stuff Like That   179
Now That's Customer Service   180
I'd Tip My Hat to You, But . . .   183
This He-Man Is a Hero a Mother Could Love   185
'Supply and Consume' Economist Goes to the
    'BIG' Store   187
Road of Life Is Paved with Car Pools   189
Sporting Events Keep Cupboards Stocked   191
Monkee Business Brings Together Mother's,
    Children's Generations   193
Today's Finds, Tomorrow's Garage Sale Items   195
VCR Family Hits Replay Button   197
Some Horning In Is Appreciated   199

10 TRIPS AND SLIP UPS
You Can't Get There From Here   203
Cavanaughs Go to Washington   205
Kitty with the Urge to Roam is as Much Trouble
    as a Child   208
Few Medals Given in Parent Marathon   210
Counting the Miles on Road to Vacation   212
Siblings, Offspring Equal a Houseful   214
Storm Follows Blizzard of Warnings   216
Travelers Take in Sights, Seafood   218

11 LESSONS LEARNED
Friends of Parents' Age 'Accept Us as We Are'   223
'How Lucky to Have Such Friends'   225
Reunion 'War Stories' Include Vietnam   227

Introduction

Grandma Hardt Was Really Something

Grandma lived with us. She moved in after I was born to help out my mom. I was the third child born in as many years. Well, she stayed until she died. Maybe it was because the next ten years brought five more babies into our house or maybe it was because we loved her and she loved us and we needed each other. After all, she was our grandma and we were her grandchildren.

The last time I saw Grandma she was in the hospital. I don't even remember what was wrong with her but I do remember that the medicine was making her act goofy. I had just got engaged and was home for Easter vacation to share the good news. She knew John and was very fond of him.

What was to be our last conversation was about him. She wondered aloud if John knew what was in store for him. When I asked her why she thought that, she groggily replied, "Well, you're so silly."

I shook my head in dismay, kissed her good-bye, and left the hospital. The most pressing thing on my mind was choosing between two wedding china patterns. She died a week after I returned to school. I was very shocked. It never occurred to me that she was going to die.

That was ten years ago this month. I think of her all the time. She was really something. Her name was Della Hardt. I often called her Della. She thought that was OK. When I think about her, I mostly think of all the fun times we had, because she was a fun person. But sometimes I think about how little I really related to her life. It makes me feel sad and guilty, although Grandma would never want me to. Maybe it was because I was young; I hope it wasn't because I wasn't interested.

Her life was difficult, even tragic. Two of her babies died as toddlers and when she was about thirty-eight my grandfather died, leaving her on the farm to raise my mother and two sons alone. Even though she was a young woman when this happened, she never remarried. Around her 70th year, in confession, a priest asked why, to which she replied, "No one ever asked me."

Her life during the Depression was probably pretty trying, but the only story she ever related about it was one about getting a permanent – or should I say a marcel, the permanent wave of the '30s. They would yank her hair so much hooking it up to the curling machine that when they were through she had such a headache she had to retire to bed. By the time she recovered, the hairdo was ruined.

I loved that story. She used to tell it to Bonnie (my sister) and me as we walked her home through the snow from Mrs. Morris' beauty shop. She had a standing appointment on Thursday for a shampoo and pin curl set.

Bonnie and I did a lot of things with Grandma. She took us to the movies and out to dinner and we laughed a lot. Della had great insight into human nature, especially our neighbors. They were great story material.

One of the best is about Grandma's new car. She always had a car. As she was taking it out for a drive she asked Marian, a kitty-cornered neighbor who was working in her rose garden, if she wouldn't like to ride along. Marian declined. "No, Della, I can't. I think I'm going to die tonight."

"That's OK, I'll have you back in plenty of time," Grandma said, "I don't like to drive after dark."

Grandma sewed for us. She also mended things, took them in, let them out, and in the era of the miniskirt she did a lot of shortening. She never raised her eyebrows at the diminishing skirts. All she ever said was, "Just mark the hem, I'll make them as short as you want. You're the one running around half dressed, not me."

Making a nice appearance was important to Grandma. Whenever she was going out she'd like to be reassured that she looked nice.

"Is my dress all right?" "What about my necklace, does it match?" I'd always offer the appropriate reassurance and at the same time wonder what difference it made . . . In my world, if you were over 30 you were over the hill and should no longer concern yourself about appearances.

Grandma was right. I was silly and she'd be glad to know that I am still silly, but now I'm mature, too. Unfortunately, she's not here to see that John has been able to put up with me. She would be happy for me and she would love to hold all my babies. And she would be happy that now I know that she wasn't just a Grandma, but a person, too.

Why did it take so long?

May 3, 1979

1 • LET'S TALK ABOUT ME

Life's Little Headaches Are Put in Perspective

Things weren't going well that day. The air conditioning wasn't working and the house was humid enough to grow exotic flowers. The upstairs shower was leaking into the kitchen, the ceiling was on the verge of caving in, and my toes still hurt from having Machaela drop the church kneeler on my foot.

I would have liked to run away. But I had no car; it was at the gas station for a new battery. I certainly would have no money after I paid my repair bills.

Then I got into a conversation with one of the repairmen. Seven-month-old Michael was sitting on the floor and the plumber commented on how cute he was. "He reminds me of one of my boys," he said. "He was a chubby baby, too, but he could really get around. He walked when he was only nine months."

He went on to tell me about his grandchildren but his thoughts returned to his son who resembled Michael . . . "We lost him." I expressed my sympathy and asked when it happened. "Two years ago at age 28 he died of cancer."

As he stood there telling me this, he was looking at Michael, and yet he seemed to be seeing his own son. His face filled with sadness. It was a look every parent hopes never to experience.

All of a sudden a hot house, a dead battery, a leaky ceiling and a sore foot lost significance on the list of life's problems. What instantly seemed important was my beautiful healthy baby and his equally beautiful and healthy brothers and sisters.

I decided that next time when instead of getting ready for bed Maureen and Machaela run up and down the hall naked saying they have sexy legs while Johnny chases them with a toilet plunger stuck to his stomach, I'm going to think it's funny instead of being frustrated that they are still up.

As a matter of fact, I've been laughing more when the house is a mess. I was only cheerful when the house was clean and when it was a mess, watch out. I decided I didn't want my children growing up thinking their mom liked a clean house more than I liked them.

Before long this philosophical attitude will probably wear off but when it does, something else will happen to shake up my perspective. For my sake, I hope it does because when I think back on these years, I want to smile.

September 21, 1983

Rustling of Mice Makes a Strong Mother Feel Trapped Like a Rat

I had thought of myself as a modern woman who is capable, self-sufficient, independent, smart – all in all a wonderful person, someone who faces a crisis and manages.

That thought is no longer necessarily true. My self-image was destroyed the morning a mouse ran across my kitchen floor.

I know, I know. The poor little mouse is more afraid of me. After all, I'm quite a bit bigger.

Horan

But I can't help it. Having a mouse, or as it turned out, mice, in the house caused me to fall apart.

The day after the intruder made his presence known, my husband went out of town on business. I thought he should have canceled the trip.

I could handle the seven children, a jammed disposal, a dead car battery – all the usual things that happen when husbands aren't available – but I couldn't handle mice.

4

After spending a day in denial, I decided to take action and quizzed everyone for a solution to mice. I was told that if I used traps set with peanut butter, the extermination would be a snap (pun intended).

After purchasing the traps, my involvement ceased. I gave them to Patrick, my 12-year-old, and had him set one in the bread drawer. That appeared to be the mouse's headquarters, judging from the gnawed plastic bread bags and chewed pieces of bread.

The next few mornings, before I went downstairs, I had the kids check the drawer to see whether the coast was clear. Waking up to a recently departed mouse trapped in my bread drawer was an experience I preferred to miss.

Before the bread-drawer visitor was evicted, however, the theory that there's never just one mouse in the house proved correct. One evening as I was getting the kids ready for bed, we discovered what became known as the upstairs mouse.

He had a long tail. This fact became significant a few days later, when I was traveling from room to room collecting dirty clothes.

I tossed the clothes on the floor of the laundry room, ran down the hall to tuck the girls in bed, and then came back a moment later. I scooped up the clothes only to have a mouse jump out of the pile. My reaction could most likely be described as an excellent cardiovascular workout.

After this incident, "jumpy" would best describe my frame of mind. I never knew when I would be face to face or toe to tail with a mouse.

One morning, I was leaning over making Johnny's bed when I felt a rustling along the cuff of my pant leg. It was a mouse. He ran out of the room, and I jumped on top of the bed.

We set a trap under the bed.

The next day I stepped on it.

Opening drawers in the kitchen and doing laundry involved a major mustering of courage. I never got out of bed until I put on my slippers.

After I endured several days of the heebie-jeebies, the peanut butter lure proved effective. One morning the kids ran upstairs all excited to report that we had won the battle of the bread drawer. Once Patrick disposed of the evidence, I went downstairs.

The next morning, my young exterminators gave me a good news-bad news story.

The good news was the capture of the upstairs mouse. The bad news was that he had a short tail. The washing-machine coast was still not clear.

Well, all-out trap setting continued until I felt assured that all the residents of our house were named Cavanaugh.

Despite my aversion to sharing my home with mice, the whole experience made me feel bad.

I wish I could have been more hospitable; after all, it was cold outside, and the little mice just wanted to be warm. It seems extreme that killing them is the only way they get the message that they aren't welcome.

Maybe if they had better manners . . . and didn't chew up our bread . . . and weren't always darting out of closets or out from under cabinets scaring me . . . I might let them stay.

On the other hand, it is my house!

April 17, 1985

. . . .

Sleepless Night Hits High Gear

Last night was one of those nights.

I couldn't sleep. My mind was entered in the Indianapolis 500 of bedtime. It was racing down the road of wakefulness, making pit stops at any and every possible line of thought.

When this occurs, I completely exhaust one subject before the wheels of the cerebral cavity peel out and are off to a new one. One thought leads to another.

I could be in bed thinking that tomorrow I'm going to the library but realize that first I have to find the books. Then I think, a page in one book got ripped. I'll have to repair it first.

I wonder if we have any tape. Probably not any that I can find. I can never find anything when I need it. I still haven't found a nail clippers, and the boys' fingernails are filthy.

And their hair is so long. I've got to get them in to have haircuts. I wonder if long hair on boys will come back in style?

I wonder if I should let my hair grow long. I saw someone in a movie with a hairdo I liked. I also liked an outfit the movie star was wearing. I'd like to find one similar to it but in a different color.

Periodically there's a lull on the midnight run when I look at the clock, shudder, flip over on my other side, kick a leg out from under the covers and flop it on top of the quilt, grab my hair at the roots with one hand and drop the other arm across my forehead, all the while muttering, "I've got to get some sleep or tomorrow I'll be as useful as an abandoned and cracked-up stock car."

This lecture to myself doesn't do any good, other than to give the computer disc of the mind another file to call up and inventory.

Usually the thoughts of the night aren't useful for any purpose other than keeping me awake.

One night I spent what seemed like hours mentally remodeling and reorganizing a department store in Walworth, WI. Although I have absolutely nothing to do with the store except to occasionally shop there when I visit Wisconsin, that night I felt compelled to revamp the business.

When I finished, I had mentally spent thousands of dollars face-lifting the exterior of the building and showcasing the store's interior.

I had arranged a gigantic sidewalk sale to eliminate all their existing merchandise, and hired a new team of buyers and sent them off to buy new merchandise at what I considered more with-it clothing markets.

This scenario unfolded as my late night scanner was reviewing all the bargains I had ever purchased, and I was wondering why no one ever wore the bathing suit I bought at that store's "buy one at regular price and get the second one for a dollar" sale.

Most of my wheel-spinning is not so imaginative. Lots of it is an express train through my finances, about the lots of money I spend and lots of money I need to pay lots of my bills. Or even more frequently, my wakefulness is a roller coaster ride covering the ups and downs of child rearing.

As tiring as a night of mental road running is, it is even worse when one of my children has this problem, because none of them will want to be alone. Usually I'll be comfortably knocked out with not a dream in my head when I sense someone entering my sleep zone.

"Mom, Mom," the voice says.

I'm dreaming, I tell myself. I'm not going to move and it will be over.

It isn't. A hand is felt tapping on my shoulder.

"Mom, I can't sleep," the voice that goes with that hand says to me.

"Go back to your room and count sheep," I tell the voice.

"I tried doing that. I counted to the highest number I know and I'm still awake."

The child continues, "I keep thinking what it would be like to have dinosaurs as next-door neighbors. Would we play with their kid dinosaurs and would they go to school with us?"

"Probably you'd do both," I mumble. "Go back to bed."

Just as I'm sinking blissfully back into a deep sleep, the tapping hand is back. "Mom, I still can't sleep. I keep wondering if for my birthday we could get a space shuttle launch pad built in the backyard."

"Your birthday is not for five months," I answer. "Go back to bed and say the rosary."

Usually this works, but it is too late because now I'm awake and thinking, "What would it be like to have dinosaurs for neighbors?"

September 14, 1988

Frantic Mom Dressed to Kill

"Mom," Maureen said, "How come you always write about everyone's fits but you never say anything about the way you act?"

"That's because I'm perfect," I answered.

"Does someone who's perfect go storming up and down the hall, wearing a slip, holding a curling iron, slamming doors and yelling, 'Why do things like this always happen?' "

"Oh, that? I was nervous."

"It looked like a fit to me," Maureen responded.

"Yeah," Colleen, the actress, joined in. "If I put on a performance like that, you'd accuse me of thinking I was on stage. You can throw a fit as good or even better than Machaela."

"I'm not a big fit-thrower at all – compared to John," Machaela added.

It is true I was on a rampage that morning, but I was beyond even my wit's end. I had been invited to speak at the mother-son Mass and breakfast for Patrick's school, Creighton Prep. I was honored to be asked but a bit apprehensive about what to say to such a large group of young men and their moms.

This engagement was scheduled after an unusually tumultuous week. I was living for the moment. And as each moment presented itself, if I was ready I handled it, and if I wasn't, I'd panic first, then somehow get through it.

On the morning of my speech, I felt "sort of" in control.

I had retrieved and collected my thoughts from the various dumping sites in my mind. I had figured out what I should wear and it was even back from the cleaners, and I had the kids all situated.

I had Patrick out of bed and had picked out clothes for him that I thought would be appropriate for the occasion.

All I had to do was get myself dressed. I was feeling almost relaxed.

"Chances are good that I'm going to get through this," I thought. No such luck.

My hair, which had looked fine and dandy for my previous day's events, probably also would have passed a grooming test if that morning it could have been touched up with my electric rollers.

Otherwise, I would look as if I just removed the nylon stocking from over my head after an all-night spree of gas station holdups.

The fit began when I ran to Colleen's room and woke her up. "Colleen, you've got to help me. My electric curlers won't heat up and my hair looks horrible."

"Your hair doesn't look bad," she said, but she didn't even have her eyes open.

"How can you tell? It's half set with hot curlers except they aren't hot. Get the curling iron and come to my room."

"Calm down, Mom, and put on your dress while this thing heats up," Colleen said as she plugged in the curling iron.

"I can't calm down. I'm going to look awful and everyone will see me because I'm the speaker."

As I continued my ranting and raving, several little folks appeared in my room to see what was going on. Maureen ushered them out, saying, "Mom has a problem with her head."

In the meantime, Colleen was trying to curl my hair but it wasn't working. I had too much hair and too little time. Then Patrick came in half-dressed.

"How come you are not ready? You make me so mad," I said to him with blood-vessel-breaking gusto.

"Gee, that is not a very nice way to talk to your son right before we go to a mom-son thing."

"Get out of here," I screamed.

"Dad's shirt you want me to wear is too small."

"What?" I flew over to the dad's closet, the curling iron flew out of Colleen's hand, and another shirt flew through the air to Patrick. "Make this one fit."

Later that day, when the speech was over and I was back at home breathing a sigh of relief, Maureen asked one of Patrick's friends who was at the breakfast how I did.

When he said I did fine, she wondered out loud: "Did anyone say anything about her hair?"

November 2, 1988

Writing a Column is Better Than Being Ann Landers

When a couple of Colleen's friends were over, we started talking about the search for Ann Landers' successor.

It seems Ann is doing some newspaper hopping. She took her column from the *Chicago Sun-Times* to the *Chicago Tribune*, so the *Sun-Times* is searching for a new advice columnist to fill Ann's space.

"You should get her job," one of the girls suggested to me.

"You already are good at giving advice," another friend added.

"That's for sure," Colleen said. "You are always telling me what I should do."

I shook my head no to these suggestions. I wouldn't accept Ann Landers' job at the *Sun-Times* – although it hasn't been offered to me – because I don't want to hear about other peoples' problems.

I have enough problems of my own. I want people to listen to my problems. That's the benefit of writing this column. I get to air all my gripes under the guise of somewhat clever storytelling.

I'm always composing letters in my mind that I could write to Ann Landers but never do. How do you think all my friends to whom I owe letters would feel if they thought I'd taken the time to write to Ann Landers instead of dropping them a friendly line?

If I did write to Ann, this is what I would say, and since I have been a constant reader of Ann Landers, I think I can safely guess how she would respond:

Dear Ann Landers,

I'm a busy woman who is always trying to do two things at once. When I leave the house to go someplace, I don't have time to comb my hair and put on lipstick.

I use stop signs and stop lights en route as occasions to groom myself, but there's always some impatient oaf, usually a man, who honks his horn because the light has changed and I haven't driven off. This startles me and I get rattled and smear my lipstick.

Signed, What's a Girl to Do?

I bet Ann couldn't give me an answer for that one because she probably is perfectly groomed at all times and doesn't do touchups in her car. So I'll answer the letter.

Dear What's,

Throw the car into reverse and step on the gas. A guy who doesn't appreciate a woman's basic needs should have his fenders altered.

Dear Ann,

My 14-year-old son's favorite pair of tennis shoes is completely torn up, yet he insists on wearing them. He can't possibly walk comfortably in them. Do you think that's why he's always sitting around watching TV and eating bowls of cereal?

Signed, Mother of Shoe Worn

Dear Mom,

That boy needs counseling and you need to quit buying cereal. You are only feeding his weakness.

Dear Ann Landers,

Ask your experts if there is a spray I can spray on my garbage on trash day so the four-legged ones will find it too disgusting to tip over and rip up.

Signed, Trashed Up Yard

Dear Trashed,

I don't answer such trashy questions.

Dear Ann,

Last night I dreamed I wasn't aging gracefully. Do you think I should start using Oil of Olay?

Signed, Wrinkles Pending

Dear Wrinkles,

You need counseling. Oil of Olay won't do anything for your guilty conscience.

Dear Ann Landers,

How come getting up early to work is considered admirable, but staying up late to do the same thing is considered decadent?

Signed, Wondering

Dear Wondering,

I'm wondering why you wonder such things. You should write a letter to that friend you have been neglecting. Maybe she'll have some answers for you.

April 22, 1987

Ann Landers
Chicago Tribune
435 North Michigan Avenue
Chicago, Illinois 60611

April 27, 1987

Kate Cavanaugh
Omaha World-Herald
World Herald Square
14th and Dodge
Omaha, NE 68102

Dear Kate Cavanaugh:

I received several copies of your column.

If you don't want to hear about people's problems, it's just as well that you didn't apply for the job. Too bad, though - I think you might have won it!

All best,

Ann Landers

AL/ls

Fashion is Nice, But a Good Bargain is Better

"Kelly and her mom have a preppy style," Colleen said. "You know, they wear all those really cool sweaters and nice pants."

"Yeah, that's right," Maureen said. "And Allison's mom has a style all her own."

"She wears the best stuff I've every seen," Colleen agreed.

"Your Aunt Cathie's friend has a glamorous style," family friend Michelle added.

In the upstairs hallway in front of the mirror, we were having a discussion on fashion and style.

"How would you describe my style?" I asked as I preened at my reflection, expecting an answer describing a combination of pizazz, glamour and good taste.

Instead, Colleen Sr., our college student helper, offered this: "Don't you have a buy-it-on-sale-and-wear-it style?"

"What is that supposed to mean?" I asked the group, which was doubled over in laughter.

"Whenever you show us what you bought on a shopping outing, the first thing you mention is how much the price of the item was discounted," Colleen Sr. said. "You are more excited about the money you saved than what you bought."

"At the end of last summer, when you bought that dress for two dollars, we thought you'd never stop talking about what a great deal it was, especially since it has the French label in it."

"Well, it was a good deal, and it paid for itself right away because Colleen wore it to play practice that night, and I wore it the next day when I met friends for coffee."

"And I suppose you told them all about how cheap it was just like you told me to brag about your shopping skills at rehearsal," Colleen Jr. said.

"As a matter of fact, I did, and they were impressed as most people are when you tell them about a good deal."

Those girls are right about me. I can't stand to buy anything unless it is on sale. I tell myself I can't afford an item and don't need it, but if it's marked down, suddenly my purchasing power appears and takes charge, literally and figuratively. For me, passing up a bargain would be like Bonnie and Clyde passing through a town without holding up the bank.

The other day I ran into a friend when I was traveling about town searching for a wet vacuum to suck up the two to three inches of water that had flooded my basement. She asked me to go with her to a sale at a very nice ladies store. "There will be big markdowns," she promised.

She didn't need to say more. I immediately dismissed my water problems until later, rationalizing that the job would be easier when some of the water had evaporated, and I was off to the sale.

The bigger the markdown, the happier I am.

"Clearance" has become one of my favorite words, as has the phrase "50 percent off lowest marked price." If an article of clothing doesn't have at least one red line through its original price tag, or isn't hanging on a special sale rack, it probably never will make its way out of the store in my possession. At these moments, I am so happy I even can instantaneously figure out in my head how much of a good deal I'm getting.

However, I have to admit that I'm not always as savvy as I purport to be.

Occasionally, I'll find a dress that has a price tag that is too good to be true, but the dress will look even better with just the right belt or scarf. So I set off searching for it and, of course, it costs three times what the dress does. And, of course, I buy it anyway.

After all, I have to spend all the money I've saved somewhere.

November 30, 1988

Gas Gauge Hovering on Empty, But Kate's Late

The needle on the car's gas gauge is teetering on big "E" and I am a bit nervous.

"I should stop and fill up my tank," I think, but if I do I'll be even later than I already am for my hair appointment, and it might be canceled and I can't go another day without a trim. So I hope I can go a few more miles with very little gas, because I'm opting to risk running out.

Croy

Things brighten as we go up hill and the gauge registers at about the one-sixteenth mark. I'm in good shape; I won't even need to buy gas on the way home. Now we are on level ground and the gauge is teetering around "E" again.

Uh-oh. We're going downhill and so is the gas gauge. I wish I had worn more comfortable walking shoes. I may be hiking to a gas station.

Whew! I made it. After the haircut I'm going directly to a gas station – if I can get the car running again.

Why am I always in this predicament? Whenever I'm in a hurry, I'm out or almost out of gasoline, and when I'm not in a hurry I don't need gas.

Of course, I never think I need gas until the gauge registers below one-thirty-second of a tank. Oftentimes I just can't get around to buying gas. Yesterday I drove car pools and I noticed I was entering the danger zone but I kept putting off stopping.

"I'll wait until after I cash a check so I can pay in cash and get the discount," I thought.

Later when I was driving again, I decided to skip the gas pumping because it was too cold outside and I didn't have my gloves.

"I'll wait until I pass that cheaper price station that pumps for you," I thought, but I wasn't going that way.

Then last night I drove the whole crowd to skating and safely back home again and it never occurred to me to look at the gas gauge. My fairy godmother must have poured some of her magic dust into my tank to get us home. But today she is saying I can only get so much mileage from those gasoline fumes. "Go to a gas station!"

Another peculiarity I have about gassing up is that when we are traveling I never want to stop until we are at the desperation point.

I figure the longer we go without filling up, the farther we can go before the next stop.

I'm one of those no-fun people who never likes to stop on trips. I want to get where I'm going, and a bunch of gas station stops only prolongs the agony. Plus, isn't it fun to see how far you can get on one tank of gas?

Fortunately, good sense – and traveling with kids – puts a damper on such an adventuresome idea. I don't think I'd like hiking down the Interstate in search of a gas station.

That doesn't mean I've never run out of gas.

We had a car once that didn't have a working gas gauge. It also didn't have a parking gear. That went out Thanksgiving Day, 1971, when one of my nine brothers-in-law – I won't name names – threw the car into park before it was completely stopped and ran into our house to watch on television what he was hearing on the car radio: Nebraska's Johnny Rodgers running long for that famous touchdown against Oklahoma.

The gauge on this early marriage car always said full, but the tank never was.

Our plan was to try to remember the mileage on the speedometer and then add the number of gallons pumped in the car times the number of miles per gallon the car would travel.

This was pure speculation since we never got around to accurately figuring the mileage.

You probably are not surprised to hear that this system seldom worked. It was confusing.

Was the mileage 80,230 or 80,320? Did we put in 10 gallons of gas, or was it $10 worth? Does the mileage differ if we drive more in town or on the highway?

I could never keep these numbers straight and John never seemed to care. Our solution then was to keep an empty gas can in the car at all times. I hope I don't end up wishing I had one today.

January 20, 1988

Lefties Elbowed in a Right-Handed World

I've discovered one more area where I'm the victim of discrimination. That's right. Me, the suburban housewife.

You probably weren't aware of it, but I'm one of the downtrodden of the world, the elbowed, the neglected members of society.

OK, OK, I'm overreacting, but it's not easy being left-handed. Let's face it (or should I say, let's hand it), this is a right-handed world, and we lefties are left to our devices – right-handed ones.

Anyway, on to the latest slight to us second-class folk. You know how it has become fashionable to accessorize clothing with a pin or a brooch? Well, the designers of these items must be right-handed.

The clasp on the back of the pin is situated so only a right-handed person can put it on. If I pin it on a sweater with my left hand, it's upside down.

Writing and eating are probably the most challenging problems for a leftie.

Many left-handed writers use what is known as overhand. I do. I think I do this because in handwriting class my paper was slanted to the left, just as my right-handed classmates' paper.

The problem with this style of writing, in addition to smearing the ink with the side of my hand, is that it's awkward.

When I was in school, note-taking was difficult in a classroom filled with right-sided desks.

Occasionally there would be a left-handed desk, but invariably a right-handed person would plop down in it and then complain about not being able to write.

Another of my gripes is spiral notebooks. If the spiral is on top of the notebook, I turn the notebook upside down.

Then there's the clipboard. When the doctor's office asks you to fill out forms, they hand you the papers on a clipboard. For lefties, the clip gets in the way. So despite the doctor's good intentions, we still write on our laps – overhanded, naturally.

Lefties are often referred to as awkward, which is exactly how I feel when I confront a buffet line at a party. Invariably the serving pieces are set to the right of the serving dishes.

I bet you've never seen a left-handed person serving punch at a wedding. If you did, more punch was spilled than poured. Punch ladles are as far to the right as Jerry Falwell and just about as stubborn.

Not only is the handle shaped for the right-handed, the bowl is situated for right-handed pouring. There's no way a leftie can use it without undergoing some contortions.

Another moment of panic is when I find my seat at a long dinner table and discover I'm seated between two other diners. I immediately get that straitjacket feeling and wonder how I'll cut my food without elbowing my dinner companion. Usually I vie with other lefties for the seat at the left end.

As you probably have guessed, I don't think we lefties get any respect. Even the word left has some negative connotations, whereas right is so . . . right.

For example, "he's way out in left field" is derogatory, but "he's right on target" is positive.

Wouldn't you rather be right than left behind? What about left-handed invitations, or having politics that are left of center (of course, I think that's fine) instead of right wing?

Being left-handed isn't always a problem. I like being different. I think lefties are more observant. I always observe other left-handers.

There are more of us than you'd expect. Left-handedness can be an advantage in sports. It's a shame I don't have more athletic prowess, so this could be to my advantage. Left-handers are almost always creative. I am. I created two left-handed sons.

January 14, 1987

'Wonder Years' for Teens, 'Worry Years' for Parents

At the beginning of the new year 10 years ago, I had three little children with the fourth expected any minute. It didn't seem possible that life could be any more hectic or that the children's demand on my time could be greater.

But all the time I would hear, "Wait until they are teenagers." It was always said by parents of teenagers in a tone of voice so ominous that it suggested living through the teenage years would be like walking through a mine field, with minimal hopes of survival.

I didn't have to wait long to have teenagers. Before I had a chance to really get the hang of mothering pre-schoolers, I had high schoolers. These high-schoolers are wonderful people just as they were wonderful grade-school kids, toddlers and babies. They aren't the problem, their age is.

Teenagers want to do things that are dangerous, that don't seem sensible (at least to parents), and that parents just aren't ready for them to do.

What worries most parents is that they remember doing the same things, and they know there is something to worry about.

The sole aim of the parents of teenagers is to usher their children through these years in one piece. Whenever, I'm out for the evening, a sudden pang of terror grips me: "Did I ask my teenagers all the right questions about their evening plans? Did I make all the guidelines and curfews clear so later they can't say, 'Oh, I didn't know I wasn't supposed to go there.' "

I look around the room, which is often filled with people of my vintage and tell myself to calm down, "You are surrounded by a houseful of people who survived the teenage years," I tell myself, "The percentages are in your favor." That helps me but still. . . .

My suggestion for weekend activities for the high school age crowd is to invite a few friends over and I'll teach them to play Bridge. I'm always looking for partners.

The teens don't think much of this plan – it's not nearly risky enough. It is much more exciting to be driving around with no definite destination, although that's not what they told Mom and Dad, who think they are at a party. The kids were at the party, but they left because it was boring and the parents were home, which is exactly the reason Mom and Dad wanted their teenagers there.

Adding to the teen's adventure for the evening is the driver, who finally passed his driver's test the previous week on the third try. On his first try he took out a couple of pedestrians. On his second try he made a left turn on red, even though he knew the law allows only a right turn on red. He gets his right and left mixed up.

What it all comes down to is worry. Lots of it. Teen-age years are the worry years. Most of the worrying is done late at night while parents are also waiting for the teenagers to come home and wondering if they will return unscathed physically, emotionally, and legally.

If they are late, the worrying automatically kicks into overdrive. If I'm in bed, I get up and stare out the window. My heart inflates as every car travels up the street and deflates when it continues by the house. If too much time passes, I go back downstairs to sit in the dark, staring alternately at the clock and out the window.

Between the times that I'm thinking about the worst scenario for why they are late, I plan what I'm going to do to them when they do arrive home. Should I be hysterical? Calm? Should I pour on the guilt? I can never make up my mind, so I go back to praying the rosary for a safe return.

Finally, all's well. The evening's errant ones appear fortified with excuses but I'm too overjoyed to listen. Now I can go to bed.

Inevitably, before my head sinks all the way into the pillow, my mother's words to me during one of my teenage summers comes flashing into the dark. "But I do worry," she said, even though I told her not to. She also told me, "Come home earlier so I can get some sleep." I hear you, Mom! Boy do I ever hear you!

January 18, 1989

'What Do I Owe You?' Is Not a Simple Question

What is high finance?

Is it what is depicted in the movie "Wall Street"? The president reporting to the nation on the complexities of the new tax bill? Donald Trump putting together a complicated real estate deal in New York City?

Croy

Or is it six women settling up the check after a $33.84 restaurant luncheon?

I often hang out with a group of female friends from my school days. The subject of money invariably emerges whenever we get together. Negotiations are begun, haggling continues, a deal is struck, money changes hands and all involved are satisfied that a fair compromise has been attained.

Isn't this what goes on in the board rooms of the corporations of America?

The only difference is they may be dealing with $20 million and we are negotiating the fate of something under a $20 bill, small but coveted hunks of money usually acquired at grocery stores when the check written exceeds the tab total because it is an odd amount.

Who wants to register $37.63 in the checkbook when it's so much neater to subtract $50 and have $12.37 in mad money to pay for Brownie dues, roller skate rental and school lunches?

One of our recent get-togethers was a birthday celebration. We discussed getting a gift (negotiations had begun). After much discussion (the haggling), one of the group had an idea for an appropriate gift, so she became the designated purchaser (the deal was struck), with plans to be reimbursed at the party (money will change hands) and the birthday girl would be delighted (satisfaction all around).

During the course of the event everyone sidled up to the shopper and in a hushed voice – after all, the giftee has to be surprised – asked, "What do I owe you?"

But it is never that simple. First old debts have to be settled and suddenly all secrecy is tossed aside.

I'll be all set up to pay my share, then my friend who did the shopping – we'll call her Gladiola – will say, "Don't pay me because I still owe you for the Girl Scout cookies."

That's right. "But it was only $5," I say.

Petunia, standing checkbook in hand, says, "Why don't I make up the difference because you gave my son money for lunch the other day when you drove car pool."

When Rose attempts to put in her contribution, Iris puts the skids on it: "You don't owe anything."

"She's right," the rest of the bouquet agree. "You brought the cake, so we'll just split the gift cost among the rest of us."

Then I say to Tulip, "Why don't I pay for you because I owe you for that cookbook your daughter's school was selling." "I almost forgot about that," she answers.

"I've got a whole bunch of those cookbooks in the car. Anyone else interested?"

"That reminds me," Magnolia sings out. "Does anyone want to go to that lecture on money management my investment club is sponsoring? I'm selling tickets."

Because this money back-and-forth has been going on for years, we think about appointing a treasurer who would tabulate who owes how much to whom for gifts, lunches, candy sales, theater tickets, flowers, our kids' walk-a-thon pledges, raffle tickets, etc. At the end of the year she would submit statements on how much we were to pay each friend.

It would probably even out and no one would owe anything.

The problem is the recorder's job would be so confusing that she'd only do it if we paid her a salary. That would be OK, as long as we could divide it six ways and it was under $20.

January 27, 1988

. . . .

Case of 'I Should Be's' Is a Daily Dilemma

Have you been wondering what I do all day? I doubt that you have, but if you were my answer would be: "I do a lot of things but not what I should be doing because I'm never doing what I should be doing."

It seems that no matter how important what I'm doing is, I can always think of something I should be doing instead.

For example, when I was going to the hospital with the distinct feeling that my baby's birth was imminent, I felt like I shouldn't go because I should be straightening up the house.

Whenever I leave the house I think I shouldn't be going because I should be mowing the lawn or scouring the bathroom or vacuuming cobwebs off the basement windows.

Don't worry, I still go and usually to a place I've been telling myself I should go when I've been doing something else.

If I'm cleaning the basement to get ready for a birthday party, I keep thinking I should be shopping for party favors. Later, when I'm out shopping for the party loot I get nervous because I should be home planning party games.

Of course, there also is the dilemma of thinking I should be in two places at once. At 5 p.m. when I'm getting dinner started, I think I should jump into the car to pick up one of the children at soccer or dancing lessons. But I also think I should get the clothes out of the dryer before they wrinkle.

If I opt for doing the laundry, then I get really nervous because I know I should hurry up and pick up the kids. But I also think I should put another load of clothes in the washer.

I get a case of the "I should be's" when I'm just hanging around keeping the home fires burning. I tell myself I should be working on some project to improve our community. Then, when I'm at a good-deed-doers meeting, I think I probably should be home doing deeds I'm supposed to be doing.

I also love going to lunch with friends. These occasions don't often occur because most of my friends also have all these things they should be doing. When we do get together, it is relaxing and fun until I decide I have to get going because I should be home doing something. Of course, when I get home after an afternoon out I never feel like doing much of anything.

Food is a continual "I should be" problem. Whenever, I eat something, I know I should be eating something else or nothing at all. If I do eat something I should be eating, I know it won't be long before I'm tempted to eat something I shouldn't.

That's why when a friend stops by for a chat, instead of sitting and visiting I feel like we should take a walk while we talk so I can walk off the brownies or ice cream I shouldn't have eaten.

When I'm having a nice dinner I would like to have a glass of wine to complement my food. But I think I should have water instead because wine will make me sleepy and I have things I should do after dinner. On the other hand, I tell myself, maybe I should have the wine because if I do I'll be relaxed enough so that all the should-be-dones are forgotten.

If I start dozing off while I'm lying on the couch reading the newspaper, I think I should go to bed. So I get off the couch and then decide I should straighten up the family room before I go upstairs.

After reading about all these dilemmas, you probably could surmise that I'm either a very complex, multi-faceted worry wart, a frazzled organizer, a nervous wreck or all of the above. But possibly I'm as normal as anyone else.

October 22, 1986

2 · NATIVITY SCENES

Bruns

Machaela Cavanaugh Was Worth Waiting For

No longer do I have to feel guilty about spending too much for a little girl's dress. Our third daughter was born Jan. 17, 1979, at 9:58 a.m. and we are thrilled with her. Now, not only does Patrick have three sisters, but I have another cuter-than-cute-itself girl to dress in hair ribbons.

The newest Cavanaugh arrived less than 12 hours after I finished writing "a column of despair" over her tardy appearance, but she was worth waiting for. She has a full head of red hair, which all sticks up, and we waver on the color of her eyes. Sometimes we think they'll be blue and at other times brown.

After waiting forever (nine and a half months) for the birth, I hesitated going to the hospital at the onset of labor. I wanted to make sure it was the real thing. My reluctance made everyone, including the doctor, nervous. He was beginning to wonder if I decided to stay home and have John deliver the baby.

Obviously he doesn't know John too well. John possesses many fine qualities and talents but midwifing is not one of them. The only delivering I would entrust to him was delivering me to the maternity floor.

Enroute to Georgetown Hospital, John struck up a subject of conversation I had broached numerous times in the past six months but got little interest. All of a sudden he became nervous because the birth was imminent and we had not chosen a name.

Well the tables were turned. I decided I had waited so long to decide on a name I could wait a few more hours to see what the baby looked like before making such a choice.

It was a sensible decision, because after her birth none of my favorites seemed to suit our precious bundle. After deliberating for a day and a half, we decided that the name Machaela was perfect, and for her middle name we chose her grandmother's maiden name of Munnelly.

We brought Machaela home last Saturday. She has been well received by her brother and sisters. So far she's a good sleeper. I think she gets exhausted on her awake times. They all want to hold her so we have to keep track of whose turn it is.

Already Maureen is a little helper. She disposes of the dirty diapers at changing times. Now if she'd only exchange her own diapers for big girls' pants. Wishful thinking, I'm afraid.

For the first time John accompanied me into the delivery room. I convinced him that it was one of life's greatest experiences, which he shouldn't miss. He was apprehensive, but agreed. He did very well and I was very happy to have him with me.

After it was all over I asked him how he felt about it. He responded that it was wonderful, he was glad that he decided to do it, but he wasn't sure he would want to do it again. My response to that was it was okay because I wasn't real sure I would want to do it again, either.

I believe that every new mother is entitled to a special first night out after having a baby and I guess President Carter agrees with me. Last night he staged a gala at the Kennedy Center in honor of China's Vice Premier Deng Xiaoping and Madame Zhuo Lin and invited us to attend.

The preparations for this event began two weeks ago just about the time that Machaela was born. The White House probably scheduled Deng's visit for this week, allowing me time to recuperate and to regain my figure to fit into a suitable gala outfit to be ready to attend. Wasn't that thoughtful of them?

You probably think that the coinciding of the vice premier's visit and my liberation from pregnancy was purely accidental. Well, even if it was, it certainly was an exciting postpartum outing.

The evening began with "A Performance of American Arts." The entertainment ranged from Rudolf Serkin, one of the finest pianists of our time, to the Harlem Globetrotters, who performed basketball aerobatics on the Opera House stage. The performance was followed by a reception of champagne and crepes in the Atrium of the Kennedy Center.

Not only was the gala a most pleasant evening, but also a historic occasion.

February 8, 1979

Hands: Independent, but Loving

As we were walking out of church Patrick put his hand in mine. It is not something he does that often anymore now that he has had his eighth birthday. He's sort of at the in-between stage where he still likes to be openly affectionate to his mom but no longer feels completely comfortable about it.

As we were walking along I started thinking about the different hands in my life. I love holding Patrick's hand. It is such a fine hand with a wide palm similar to his EE-width foot. Besides occasionally holding hands with me, Patrick's hands are involved in inventions of his own making. He's sure that he could build an elevator for our house if only he had the wood. These same hands are also hard at work making the transition from printing to script handwriting.

Colleen's hands are more readily available for holding. She's six and a half and very affectionate. She'll hold hands with me, Dad, and even Patrick when I send them on a big kids' errand. Colleen and I have lots of conversations about her fingernails. She would like to grow her nails long and have glamorous hands, but I won't let her because they are always dirty that way. I tell her that if she doesn't let me clean and trim them, people will think that no one cares about her. She doesn't understand this kind of thinking.

Maureen's little four-year-old hands are beginning to make drawings to be displayed taped on the refrigerator. Sometimes I tape them upside down which causes her great distress. I love to hold her hands and she loves to hold mine. Her hands are so sweet and little just like she is.

Machaela's hand-holding has to be done when it is Machaela's idea. I guess that decision is an undeniable right of a 20-month old baby. The times that she never seems to want to hold hands are when we are crossing a busy parking lot from the car to a store. This is usually a time for a streak of independence. Her little hands can hold so many things especially when she's going to bed. She can carry Dee and Snoopy, her dolls, and Dee's pillow and her own blanket.

Many times I have been at meetings where John is the speaker. At the time I am interested in his subject but find when it is over I haven't really heard his speech at all because I have been looking at his hands the whole time, noticing all his gestures and thinking that I would like to be holding his hands in mine right then.

That is a lot of hands to think about on the short walk out of church, but it all led to one thought. Would our new baby be healthy? Would the baby have all his fingers and toes?

I didn't have to wait long to get my answer. Our new baby was born the next morning, an 8-pound, 10 ounce red-haired boy, whom we named John Joseph Jr. I think the first question any mother asks before wondering what sex the baby is, or what color hair the baby has, is "Is the baby OK? Does he have all his fingers and toes?" We are so thrilled and thankful that we have been blessed with another healthy baby.

I now have another pair of hands to fill my heart with joy.

October 16, 1980

. . . .

Kate Has Another Man in Her Life

It happened so fast. Oh, I know it was nine and a half months, but all of a sudden it was over and it happened. I fell in love again hopelessly and forever. It is a love that I know will never waver. No matter what, it will grow stronger. Our sixth child, a 9-pound-5-ounce baby boy, Michael William, was born February 1st.

The whole time I was expecting, I loved him because he was our baby. Yet, it seemed like love in the abstract. I wondered what he would be like, what the other kids would think of him and I worried about him. Would he be healthy?

Then he arrived. The second the doctor held him up – I can't even remember if he was right side up or upside down – I began loving him just for himself.

After I checked the baby over, my thoughts traveled back to an afternoon a week before Christmas. I had some errands to do. Patrick didn't want to come along, but I made him, insisting that I needed his help with the kids.

When we were in the drugstore buying stamps and wrapping paper, I noticed Patrick examining the extension cords. I knew he was thinking how he could have used them when he and his dad hung the outdoor Christmas lights the day before.

All of a sudden so many of my motherly feelings rushed forward. Patrick seemed so grown up, yet I remembered when he was a baby. I thought he was the most wonderful baby in the world, and I loved him so much. I didn't think I would have any love left over to give another child. Luckily Colleen was born soon thereafter, and I quickly realized that love has tremendous room for expansion.

Every day in some way each of my children fills my heart with joy. Every day they also try my patience and fray my nerves. But now, when the house is quiet, I want to remember Patrick thoughtfully bringing the bassinet downstairs the day we brought the baby home from the hospital; Colleen carefully trying to lay the baby in the bassinet after she rocked him to sleep; Maureen making three trips upstairs to get everything I needed for a diaper change; Machaela patiently waiting for her turn to hold the baby until I fed him; and Johnny saying, "I love Michael William."

February 23, 1983

A note from Kate:

There is no baby story about Peter Hardt Cavanaugh, a guy who is cuter than cute itself, because he was born October 21, 1984 when I was between column writing jobs.

Two Sisters Share the Spoils of Maternity

Lake Geneva, WI. – Boy, am I popular – at least with a couple of people.

When I packed to come to my parents' lakeside summer home for an annual family gathering, I gathered play clothes for warm weather, sweatshirts for cool nights, swimsuits for everyone, one good outfit to wear to church or restaurants, the tennis rackets, the camera, the water wings and the baby stroller.

But it was my maternity clothes that have made me so popular.

I am what doctors call a grand multipara, one who has given birth several times. That means among other things, I have accumulated a substantial wardrobe in the maternity line.

Two of my sisters who are visiting are, as we say in polite company, "in the family way." And since my family is just in the way instead of on the way, I offered to give my sisters my maternity clothes.

Due to their timing, they have to share the spoils of my pregnancy labors. Luckily, there's plenty of selection.

Many women never want to invest much money to clothe themselves during what they consider a temporary condition. Even some of the women who seem to be in this temporary condition permanently are hesitant.

I, however, have been a good customer at the expectancy shops. On baby No. 5, I rationalized that it would be my last pregnancy, so I may as well go out in style.

With No. 6, I convinced myself that the expenditure was worthwhile to boost my morale. For No. 7, I just elaborated on that thinking.

My maternity wardrobe turned out to be more stylish than my non-maternity clothes.

Now, with moms-to-be Sheila and Mary Pat ready to tender an offer in the friendly takeover of my stock, I have decided it has been a sound investment.

But how should the sale be accomplished? I suggested an auction – Mary Pat and Sheila could write down all the nice things they could do for me, and I would select from their lists. As I selected, they could choose a garment.

Then Barbara, another sister, became involved. "Mary Pat, didn't you spend quite an extended time in Omaha and Washington babysitting for some little redheads?"

And "Sheila, haven't you made a few travel arrangements for the Cavanaughs?" (Sheila's a travel agent.)

As the realization set in that past favors might outweigh my stack of clothes, Barbara told me, "I think you'll have to go shopping."

I decided the recipients could settle it between themselves.

So Mary Pat made piles on the picnic table according to categories – nice dresses, casual things and work clothes. She said that since I had on my bathing suit, I could model the clothes.

We had such a fun time – I was especially enjoying myself because, as I told them, it was the last time I'd ever be dressed like that.

To which they said, "Sure, and my baby will always sleep through the night."

I hope they have triplets.

August 28, 1985

She Never Expected To Be Expecting Again

A few weeks ago at my doctor's office, the nurse asked, "When are you going to tell your readers about the baby? Don't you think they'll wonder if suddenly in August you add another name to the cast of characters in your column?"

I decided Nurse June was probably right – I should make you aware of my delicate condition. Cavanaugh Baby No. 8 is expected in mid-August. Although we thought seven was a lucky number for a family and planned to leave it at that, we discovered last winter that our luck was increasing.

Once we medically established that another Cavanaugh had germinated, John and I kept the news to ourselves until my fine – tuned body began slipping into the shape in which it hums best. This required a change in wardrobe.

Ordinarily that means a trip to the spare closet where my maternity clothes hang, having their biennial rest. But you may recall that last summer I gave the clothes to my two expectant sisters, because I never expected to be expecting again.

I planned that all the clothes I would buy from then on would have waistlines. I planned wrong. Or maybe it's that I never planned at all.

So what's a girl to do? Well, I went out and bought a bunch of new clothes. I suppose you're thinking, "that doesn't make sense, to spend money on clothes she'll only wear a few months."

That may be the case, but having eight children already proves I don't have a lot of sense, so I may as well enjoy my delirium fashionably.

Luckily, since I've been through this before, being pregnant is not difficult. What really gets on my nerves is the weight.

You haven't experienced humility until you've suffered through a nine-month battle with the scale in your doctor's office.

I would never consider announcing my weight in public, even if I wasn't pregnant, even if I had just returned from a 40-day fast in the desert. So you can imagine how I dread hoisting myself monthly, and then weekly, onto a doctor's scale.

Some days, I convince myself that each day I am temperate in my calorie consumption is one fewer day I'll have to deprive myself to get back my sexy shape (such as it was) after the baby is born. That good-sense approach usually lasts until about 4 p.m.

Some days, my good intentions never have a chance. I call these chocolate chip cookie or doughnut days.

This over-indulgence is justified if it happens after a doctor's appointment. Such a bender is necessary to lift my spirits when I've conscientiously been counting calories (and some days the count is high) and I still gain 3 pounds.

Health experts, I'm sure, are shaking their heads in dismay at my approach to nutrition. They are always telling pregnant women to eat from the four food groups – meals such as green vegetable sandwiches made with whole-grain bread. This would suit me fine if one more food group could be added: junk.

Instead of concerning myself with what I can or cannot eat, as opposed to what I want to eat, I should be choosing a name for the little one.

But as I sit here chewing on the ice cubes in my glass of water, the only names that come to mind are Fudge Sauce for a girl and Banana Split for a boy.

July 9, 1986

• •

Ritual of Motherhood Means Buying a New Nightgown

After eating, we decided to take a walk and look in the stores around the restaurant before going home.

The display in one shop caught my eye. Suspended from the ceiling was a silk and lace negligee, and hanging next to it was its companion morning jacket.

"Look at that nightie," I said to my friends, "Isn't it something?"

"Yes," they agreed it was. "Why don't you go in and try it on?"

"I don't think so," I laughed. "It doesn't look like something suitable for making the kids' cinnamon toast and cereal."

The outfit reminded me of something one would buy if she were planning to have a love affair in Paris or Rome, or if she played the part of the conniving other woman on a soap opera. Since neither of these circumstances was likely to occur, we continued walking.

As much as I would enjoy having something that pretty and bold in my wardrobe, I don't. The only time I buy nightgowns is when I'm going to the hospital to have a baby, which is a fairly regular occurrence for me.

Once again, my long-awaited delivery date is near, which puts me in the market for a new hospital ensemble.

After a woman gives birth, a nightgown is the first clothing she puts on that doesn't resemble the "awnings" she's been draping herself with for the last several months.

Although her figure doesn't spring back quite as quickly as a television mother's, it is a lot closer to its original form once mom and baby part company.

Therefore, it is necessary to celebrate by wearing something extra pretty when receiving compliments on the beautiful child she has produced. At least, I think it is.

So what should I get? I would like to buy something frilly and feminine like the ensemble I saw in the store window last summer, but that wouldn't be appropriate hospital wear. However, what I see in the stores that would be appropriate is so boring and unflattering.

Before I have a baby, I go on a search for just the right mix of appropriateness and style. It also has to fit.

The other day, accompanied by nine-year-old Maureen, I went on one of these shopping outings. We started going through the racks.

"How about this one?" Maureen asked as she picked out a filmy gown. "It's pretty."

"Yes, it is . . . but I don't think so," I answered.

Her next offering was reminiscent of a cancan girl's outfit. I imagined the looks I would receive from the nursery room nurse when she carried the baby into my room for a feeding.

No, the feeling I want to convey is Madonna-like (I'm referring to the Blessed Mother, not the singer), with glamorous overtones. Looking like a dancer in the follies wouldn't project that image. I hung up the red and black gown.

"Let's look over here." I pointed to another rack.

"This one is nice," I said as I held up a simple yellow number with flowers embroidered on it. "They also have it in white and in pink. Which one should I get?"

"Get the pink one, then for sure we'll have a girl and we can name her Maureen Jr.," my daughter said, cringing at the thought of having a fifth brother.

"Well, I haven't had anything in yellow in a while – maybe I'll get the yellow one. But it's pretty in white, too."

"We'll have a contest," Maureen decided as she grabbed the three sleepshirts from me and began her selection process.

"No, my feet are swelling and they hurt. Let's leave," I said.

"Here, take off your shoes," Maureen said, and before I could object I was standing barefoot after Maureen swept the shoes off my feet.

I did feel a lot better, so I kept looking. This may have been a mistake, because I ended up buying three nightgowns, the pink one Maureen wanted, a blue one in case the baby is a boy, and yellow one because I liked it.

Now I'm all ready, except for outfitting the baby's crib. Pink, blue, or yellow?

August 27, 1986

. . . .

Family Makes Room for One More

If I had been gambling a week ago Friday, I would have put my money on the number eight and won big. Even though I was too busy to go to the track, my lucky streak couldn't possibly have been more wonderful.

At 8 p.m. on August 22, I gave birth to my eighth child, an 8-pound, 8-ounce beautiful baby boy. He came into the world with a healthy body and an abundance of red hair.

The joy I felt at his arrival astounds me. Being blessed once again with a child seems like a gift only a greedy person would expect. I hoped and prayed that this would be another healthy baby and my heart is overflowing with gratitude that we received one.

It took a day and a half to decide on a name for the baby. My son Patrick had been lobbying to call him David Letterman, after the late-night TV talk show host. Colleen was putting on the pressure for Davy Jones, after one of the Monkees. My doctor suggested Ron, after President Reagan.

We vetoed all of these excellent suggestions and gave him the name Matthew Conroy. His father says Matt Cavanaugh sounds like a great name for a quarterback or a pitcher.

Matthew's four brothers and three sisters came to visit the afternoon after his birth. They arrived, accompanied by Grandma Cavanaugh, bringing flowers and candy. After washing their hands and putting on the protective gowns, each one took a turn handling the new baby while the new daddy took pictures.

As delighted as the kids were with the new baby, Matthew did have some competition for attention. My hospital bed and the box of candy also were strong attractions.

Pete was pushing the button to make the head of the bed rise. Mike was standing on the mattress and pushing the button to make the foot of the bed go down and Johnny was pushing the buttons that elevate the entire bed.

In the meantime, Maureen and Machaela were trying to get the bed's side rails to move. In case you were wondering, I wasn't in bed while all this was going on.

When the kids' hands weren't on the control buttons, they were in the candy box.

One of the hospital nurses said to me, "You and your husband sure are excited about the baby. You would think he was your first one. It's nice to know you haven't become matter-of-fact after having so many children."

After talking to the nurse, I thought that it's easier to become excited about each additional child we have. We already know that there is room in our hearts to love one more and now that Matthew Conroy has arrived, we can't wait to get to know him.

I'll let you get to know him, too.

September 9, 1986

Friends Greet New Baby, And Boy, Can They Cook

Having delicious, nutritious and elegant meals appear effortlessly on our dinner table is a fantasy I often daydream. Recently, this is a daydream come true.

When I came home from the hospital carrying our beautiful new son, Matthew, I was greeted with the news that our evening meal would be brought over by a friend, Louise.

Sure enough, later that day Louise arrived carrying a large pot, followed by her children who were carrying containers of food.

"What do you have there?" I asked, licking my lips. "It's manicotti," Louise answered as she lifted the lid to show me. "It's all set – just keep it warm in the oven until you're ready to eat. There's also salad here, Italian bread and some dessert."

When our family sat down to eat, we all agreed that having such a nice meal was a great welcome home for the new baby, even though he didn't have any of it.

The next day, we breakfasted on a fresh fruit salad and lunched on potato salad sent over by our neighbor, Jean. Dinner that evening turned into another banquet when my friend and neighbor, Kathy, and her children brought a roast beef dinner.

The following day turned out to be equally tasty when Julie arrived with a roasting pan filled with a pot roast and vegetables.

She also was accompanied by her children, who were carrying salad, wine and dessert.

This kind of treatment should have been enough to spoil me completely, but it didn't stop. Sue brought one of our favorite casseroles to put in the freezer and also a pan of sinful caramel brownies.

Claudia brought an exotic crab salad lunch for me and cookies for John and the kids, which I helped eat.

Kerry, my former nursing student helper, now a nurse and a married lady, arrived from her home in Ravenna, NE., to see the baby and to lend a hand for a few days. She lugged in a container of kolaches that she and her mother had made for us.

Whenever any of the extended Cavanaugh family comes by to take the kids off my hands, they drop off some form of nutrition.

This morning, just when I was thinking this is the day I'll have to break down and cook, Cindi arrived at my door carrying a roaster full of stew.

I always knew I had good-hearted friends and family, and it sure is nice that they are all such good cooks.

Before I get too accustomed to all this pampering, (Maureen already has; yesterday she asked, "Whose turn is it to bring over dinner tonight?") I've decided I've got to take the cure. Which means I have to stop eating so grandly if I want to fit back into my clothes.

According to articles I've read in baby magazines, new mothers shouldn't be impatient. We should allow four to six months to regain our shapes.

Well, I think like the corporate executive's wife who had made eight moves in 13 years, just as I've had eight babies in 13 years.

When she moves into each new home, she doesn't know how long she will live there before moving again, so she figures she may as well redecorate right away and enjoy her surroundings.

I feel the same way about being pregnant. I never know how long I'll be out of maternity clothes before I'll need them again, so after the baby comes I have to hurry and shape up.

That's my plan for this week and it should work – unless someone brings over more brownies. Don't you think it would be rude if I didn't help eat them?

September 17, 1986

'Happy St. Mother's Day'

I was in a hurry. I had run upstairs to change my clothes for a late afternoon meeting when I heard two-year-old Mike waking up from his nap. I went into his room, picked him up from his crib and sat down to get some hugs and loves.

This scene only lasted a few seconds because we both had things to do. I had my meeting to get to, and Mike heard the music of his favorite cartoon show coming from the downstairs television.

As he ran off in one direction I was about to turn and run off in the other, but I didn't. I stood at the top of the stairs. Watching a chubby little boy wearing rubber pants ballooning around his legs holding onto the bannister with both hands as he took one step at a time seemed at that moment like the most important thing in the world.

Unfortunately, my thinking doesn't always go that way. There are many days when watching my children becomes the least important thing. Getting the laundry done and the kitchen cleaned comes before them.

It shouldn't be that way, but sometimes it's hard for the cup of motherly love to overflow when the house is overflowing with messes.

Even when I can't see my children through the sea of debris, I can always hear them. I can't help but listen to them – and isn't listening one of the elements necessary to successful parenting?

Of course, I'm not sure that listening to Patrick tell Colleen's friend that Colleen can't come to the phone because she's outside gazing at the stars when she's standing right next to him grabbing the phone and screaming that he's a jerk is the kind of listening that the child psychologists are referring to.

I know that I should listen to what my children are saying, and I should be watching them and enjoying them and reading to them and having them read to me and playing Old Maid and Candy Land and tossing balls with them.

I want to do all those things. I want to be the devoted mother – but jeepers creepers, if I expend all my energies on listening and watching and doing for my children, I wouldn't have time to do anything for myself.

What would happen to my dreams? They didn't go out the window when I gave birth. I want to be a mother, but I also want to continue being a person – maybe even a tap dancer or a torch singer.

No one said being a mother would be easy. The only advice I received beforehand was to be sure to get a husband first.

What someone should have said was that once you have the children it's OK – even important – to develop and explore non-mothering skills. They should have added that no matter what the circumstances, you'll end up feeling guilty.

That's not necessarily fair, but it's true. You could be in the midst of negotiating world peace agreements when hovering ominously in the background would be your conscience tinged with guilt because your daughter went off to school needing a shampoo or your son had outgrown all his pants.

The trade-offs are tough in this job. I love observing the creative imagination of my two-year-old, but I'd also love to be able to leave a lipstick on the kitchen counter and not have it used as a magic marker on the living room couch.

I treasure the chance to sit in a rocking chair cuddling a little baby, but I also treasure a good night's sleep.

I realize the importance of helping a seventh grader figure out the difference between subordinate and independent clauses, but sometimes I'd rather use my analytical skills on a bridge game.

Motherhood seems to be a juggling act. When all the balls are smoothly rotating from air to hands and back again, it is life's most joyous and fulfilling experience.

But when the balls fall, or too many balls get into the act, it's a good time to watch a chubby little toddler go down the stairs.

To all mothers trying to juggle through life, I join with your children in wishing you what we at our house call "Happy St. Mother's Day."

May 8, 1985

3 • MARRIED TO A MEMBER: LIFE IN WASHINGTON DC

The Thrill of Washington Continues for Kate

After living in Washington a short time, I have learned to be prepared for the unexpected.

Recently, I drove John to the airport for what we thought would be a trip back to Nebraska. As we approached the waiting area, John was paged for a telephone call. When he returned he said, "That was the White House on the phone, the President wants me to go to India for President Ahmed's funeral with Miss Lillian and Chip Carter."

"Should I go?" he asked. "Of course you should go," I replied, "but you don't have any money or a passport."

John answered that he told them that and The White House said he didn't need to worry.

Within ten minutes a late-working White House aide opened the door to a black limousine. John climbed in. Off they went to Andrews Air Force Base and an awaiting presidential jet.

Shortly after we arrived in Washington, as we walked back to our hotel, pushing baby Maureen in her stroller, the Capitol sitting splendidly before us, John asked, "Do you think you will be happy here."

"I don't know if I can stand the excitement," I said. We laughed, feeling certain that the thrill would quickly wear off – but it hasn't.

Unquestionably, Washington is an exhilarating place and we have delighted in it. Although Jimmy Carter's inauguration was several weeks ago, I still get excited thinking about it.

John Kennedy was sworn in as President when I was in the eighth grade, and ever since, I have watched television and read in the newspaper about the oath of office and the inaugural address. I feel it is one of our country's greatest moments; a transition of great power carried out peacefully. This is an awesome event and I was there witnessing it.

As the Marine Band played "Battle Hymn of the Republic," Gerald Ford, in the closing minutes of his presidency, and Jimmy Carter, anticipating his monumental undertaking, sat next to each other talking. I couldn't help wondering what one talks about under such circumstances.

Life in Washington is different from what we are used to but we are enjoying it. I just have to remember to take my map when I go driving and allow more time to get to places.

We are renting a home in an older neighborhood of Washington. We wish we could stay here but unfortunately the owners will be returning from Florida in May.

We are flabbergasted at the high price of real estate – a good deal is $125,000 for a four-bedroom colonial style house. We are hoping we can find an Omaha type "good deal."

We do miss our good friends, the prices and conveniences of Omaha, but we hope to have the best of both places by making frequent trips back to Nebraska and by having many of our Nebraska friends visit us here.

As we go about our new life, we often think of John's father, Jack. Politics and good government meant so much to him. He was so proud of John. We know he would love to hear our tales of Washington.

March 10, 1977

Why does Jimmy Carter Envy Kate Cavanaugh?

The title of this column could be "Jimmy Carter envies Kate's leadership abilities," or "How I went bonkers on 18th and Columbia Road N.W."

Both of these events actually took place on the occasion of the New Congressional Members family picnic. I was asked to provide the entertainment. At first I thought they wanted me to tap dance (my next career), but the picnic organizers quickly informed me that they meant relay races and other games.

To do something different, I decided to be organized. I planned various relay races, gathered the necessary equipment, made up lists for the scavenger hunt, and bought prizes. I even rounded up a volunteer from The Earth Onion Woman's Theater who would come in costume to entertain the children with mask-making and mime. I put everything in the car early so I could avoid a last-minute rush. However, what would life be without last-minute rushing?

The picnic was being held from 6 p.m. until dark at Rock Creek Park. John planned to meet me there as soon as the House adjourned for the day.

At 5:30 p.m. I jammed into the car the three kids, myself and the brownies minus the frosting which Patrick and Colleen had eaten off. Then I had to pick up the volunteer clown at 18th and Columbia Road. I didn't think I'd have any problem finding her; after all, she would be standing on the street dressed as a giant ugly duckling. But it was rush hour and I went up and down more one-way streets the wrong way, made several (unknowingly, of course) illegal left-hand turns to the tune of Maureen screaming her head off and I still couldn't locate the theater. I was about to resort to screaming myself when a gas station attendant helped me after I hysterically blurted out my predicament. So I finally found my duckling whose talents were well worth the search party.

Geography lesson to be learned from this is 18th Street N.W. changes into Adams Morgan Road at the 2500 block.

When at last our entourage got to the picnic, I collapsed – not really. I was rejuvenated and had a wonderful time. It was a regular family picnic with one exception: there were park police on horseback and Secret Service men in attendance. Amy Carter was there to the delight of all the other children.

Now you are probably wondering, "Why is Jimmy Carter envious of a person like her?" Well, he isn't – but it makes good copy.

After we ate, it was time for me to provide the entertainment which included a father-child relay. No Congressman or Senator was exempt. If they had no children or their children weren't there, they borrowed one from families who had extras. This was not an easy group to manipulate. Tony Beilenson of California wondered if he should carry his sixteen-year-old or if his son should carry him. As unruly as they were, I managed to get about twenty five new members of Congress to line up and follow my orders. There were two teams and each one felt they had won the relay, so they were all happy. M & M's were given as prizes.

So now can you see why President Carter might envy my political savvy?

We had several other activities, but mostly the picnic was an opportunity for the families to get together informally and become better acquainted.

June 15, 1977

White House Picnic Makes Kate's Heart Pound

Going to the White House is a thrill. You'd have to be terribly blasé not to have a little fluttering of the heart when you walk through the White House gates. Last Thursday evening, when we attended President Carter's White House picnic, my heart not only fluttered, it pounded all evening.

President and Mrs. Carter gave a picnic for the members of Congress and their families. The House was in session a little late so the children and I came ahead of John. Patrick and Colleen were as excited about the picnic as I was.

We entered through the lovely Jacqueline Kennedy Garden. On the Presidential grass was a tent where soft drinks were served, a buffet table where the bill of fare included hamburgers, hot dogs, cole slaw and baked beans.

A huge stage was assembled so we could enjoy square dancing and a New Orleans jazz band. Colleen liked the music so much that she swayed to the blues as if she were on Bourbon Street. Clowns greeted the children and made animals from the balloons. On the lower lawn, a net was set up where teen-agers played volleyball with the Washington Redskins. There was even a hayrack which gave rides all around the grounds.

The Carters came out of the house at about 7 o'clock and remained until after dark. The President was dressed very casually. He and Mrs. Carter made sure they greeted everyone and patiently posed for pictures with everyone's baby including ours. Patrick diplomatically gave me his fudge bar stick before offering the President his sticky hand.

Hubert Humphrey was also there, looking quite well. I was delighted when he remembered meeting me in Omaha last October. It was a week previous to Maureen's birth so I was big with child. I'm sure that's why I stuck in his mind.

The ground floor of the White House was open so naturally we went in. We browsed through the Diplomatic Reception Room, the China Room and the Library where President Carter gave his first fireside cardigan sweater chat.

As we were leaving the mansion, we bumped into Chip Carter, who had just returned from a week in California. We chatted for only a few minutes because he was anxious to find his wife, Caron, and baby son, James.

All in all, it was a sparkling and memorable event.

August 11, 1977

The Campaign is Over — Oh, What a Relief It Is!

"Hello, I'm Kate Cavanaugh, John's wife. John is running for re-election to Congress. We'd appreciate your support on November 7."

"Oh, it's past November 7, the election is over, and John was reelected? That's great. I was so busy handshaking I forgot about the vote-taking."

What a relief! The campaign of 1978 is over, and I'm writing my "Letter from Washington." It's good to be back. I've missed writing, and I appreciate all the inquiries by readers who say they've missed reading my column and wondered when I would be back.

Much has happened since I last wrote. We went through a long and exciting campaign. It's a good feeling to have that behind us.

Political campaigns were not something I was exposed to growing up in St. Charles, IL. The most exciting — and also about the only — political experience I had was in 1960. John Kennedy was campaigning in St. Charles. We must have had a Republican pastor at my school, because we weren't let out early to hear him speak. But as soon as school was dismissed, my dad jammed my brothers, sisters, and several friends into his Volkswagon and raced us to the parade site.

It was there, on the corner of Third and Main, in front of Lencioni's Blue Goose Grocery, that I got to shake hands with the next president.

Believe me, it was a great thrill, especially since my only other political experience would be three years later, when I went to my high school's Christmas formal with a son of the mayor of St. Charles.

But in Omaha, it is different. At least in South Omaha, where politics is a way of life and every occasion is a political one. Church dinners are a politico's delight. The hoopla surrounding a plate of roast beef and mashed potatoes never ceases to make me wonder.

During a lively election year, in front of the church hall volunteers are handing out literature on candidates for jobs ranging from landfill overseer to the president. While waiting in line for the bill of fare, diners can read the literature, shake the candidates' hands, and peruse the walls completely decorated with political posters.

On being seated, the choices continue. The now well-informed diner can stick on his favorite candidate's sticker, file his nails with a political emory board, make a grocery list on a political tablet, put on a political rain bonnet in case of a shower of political rhetoric, light a political cigar with political matches, and finally, eat a meal set on a political placemat.

The key to a successful campaign is going out, meeting and talking to the potential voters. In order to do this, one has to go where the people are. The campaign trail leads a candidate down a path of bowling alleys, plant gates, shopping centers, union halls, country clubs, school festivals, church bazaars, meetings with senior citizens, meetings with junior citizens, and just meetings.

On one busy campaign day driving between a bake sale and a school carnival, my sister-in-law Pat and I were reminiscing about what it would be like to have a normal day where we did nothing more than stay home, fold laundry, and watch soap operas. We both agreed it would be nice, but probably not as interesting.

In a political campaign, the wide range of activities exposes one to different facets and cultures of our community. If we weren't involved in it, we might have a more tranquil lifestyle, but we'd also have a much narrower view of the world.

There are no glamour jobs in getting someone elected. John Green, a dedicated worker in our campaign, summed it up well: "At age 5, I was involved in my first campaign. I stuffed envelopes, licked them, and put stamps on them. Twenty-four years later I'm still involved in campaigns, and I'm still stuffing, licking, and stamping envelopes."

John and I feel that the success in his re-election to Congress was determined by the thousands of hours of hard work by the dedicated and enthusiastic campaign workers and volunteers. This dedication and support is tremendously heartwarming and we are very grateful.

November 16, 1978

Kate Enjoys Fairyland Evening at White House

Christmas is a-coming and the geese are getting fat – and so am I. All I want for Christmas is to be able to bend over again, be able to buckle my shoes, and not need a Caterpillar crane to raise me out of bed. However, these presents aren't scheduled to arrive until after the New Year begins.

Christmas activity is in full swing at two of Washington's White Houses. One is the White House on Pennsylvania Avenue where Jimmy and Roslyn Carter live and the other White House (with its black shutters) is where John and Kate live.

The official start of the Christmas season began Dec. 12 when President and Mrs. Carter opened the doors of the White House for the Congressional Christmas Ball.

The holiday atmosphere was unlike any I had ever seen. Upon arriving, we were greeted with Christmas carols sung by the Marine Band, brilliant red carpets, huge poinsettias, and a glass of eggnog. Upstairs the decorations were even more magnificent. Huge wreaths with red bows hung in every window, green garlands were draped over all the archways and holly, poinsettias, and red candles were bountiful. They had truly decked the halls.

The President and Mrs. Carter formed a receiving line in the Blue Room. In the center of the room is the official White House Christmas tree.

The tree, a 20-foot Veitchii Fir grown in Garrison, N.Y., was decorated with more than 2,800 miniature Victorian toys from the

Margaret Woodbury Strong Museum of Rochester, N.Y. The late Mrs. Strong hoped to create a "museum of fascination" with the things with which Victorian Americans surrounded themselves: ceramics, quilts, toys, and children's playthings. All the toys are 50 to 100 years old.

After receiving their guests, the Carters led the dancing in the East Room to the music of Peter Duchin's orchestra.

Following this fairyland evening I was brought quickly back to reality the next day when I fulfilled my motherly responsibility by selling milk and ice cream bars at Patrick's school cafeteria. Since then I have been busy readying things at the Cavanaugh White House for the approaching holiday.

Having small children around at Christmas time is especially nice. At our house each of them has a special task. Patrick is in charge of the countdown on the calendar, Colleen relays in precise detail the birth of Jesus in Bethlehem, and Maureen plays Christmas carols on the record player. Maureen is only two and not really the most logical choice for this task. However, the fact that she is two and that she thinks she should be playing the records is why she's doing it.

At this time of year I'm thankful for many things – my husband, my children, that I live in America – and when our baby's born he/she will be so young he won't care that I never bleached out the infant T-shirts stored in the attic.

We are eagerly awaiting the arrival of 1979, which we hope will bring all of you much happiness, health, and prosperity, and in addition will bring us a healthy new baby. Do you think we'll have a red-head?

December 28, 1978

Could Kate's Kitchen Be The New Sans Souci?

There's a search on in Washington for a new place in which to see and be seen. The Sans Souci, the pinnacle of "highfalutiness," is tumbling as a restaurant favorite. They have lost their maitre d'.

What reason is there to go to a restaurant whose maitre d' has departed? None! The food reportedly has been lousy for years. Without Paul, nothing is assured. What kind of entrance can you make when, upon entering, you are seated under the emergency exit?

Talk of the toppling has been swirling around Washington. Last week, *Washington Post* columnist Richard Cohen devoted his column to it. It seems Art Buchwald, the syndicated columnist and one of Sans Souci's most noted patrons, is beside himself. Without Sans Souci, where is he going to go to order the usual?

Cohen decided to help Buchwald out in his search for a new noontime hangout. Together they set out to sample Washington lunch spots. What qualities does the new "in" spot need in order to make it "in"? A maitre d' who recognizes you upon your arrival, makes sure your entrance is noted by all the other patrons, and seats you ringside.

When I read Richard Cohen's account, immediately I knew I had something to offer. I have never been to Sans Souci (the only place I go to see and be seen is the Giant Food Store), but I can imagine what it is like. Considering that, I wondered why couldn't my kitchen become the next watering hole and feed bag for the Elite? I could offer them everything that Sans Souci does, plus things that they couldn't ever possibly duplicate.

Before contacting Mr. Cohen, I decided I should plan out the motif of my restaurant to make sure it would qualify. Being the maitre d' would be no problem. I generally recognize the people who come in my front door. Nor would seating or "the usual" present any difficulties. All would be seated at the best table because there is only one in my kitchen, and the bill of fare would be peanut butter and jelly or a bologna sandwich.

The extras would be luncheon entertainment with records spun by Maureen who, joined by Colleen, dances to the music. An opportunity to hold a newborn baby – or to listen to one cry if you don't – would be another bonus. Making my restaurant even more exclusive would be its limited operation. Late openings on Monday would be necessary because I have to drive Colleen's carpool, and the place will be closed on Wednesday because I'm maitre d' of the milk and ice cream at Patrick's school cafeteria.

After establishing these criteria, I began to drum up business. I called Richard Cohen and presented him the opportunity to be my first customer. How could he turn down an invitation to be a pioneer at what was sure to become the trendy new lunch spot? We set a Thursday date, but Thursday came and so did an ice storm. We postponed until Tuesday, which turned out to be the day after the biggest Washington snowstorm in 50 years. We postponed again.

This time my illustrious guest had a hopelessly snowed-in car, so I added another fringe benefit to lunching in my kitchen – limousine service (the limousine being a Ford Maverick, chauffeured by me and liveried by four little redheads). Upon picking up Mr. Cohen I launched into one of the literary dialogues I was offering at my new salon. For a special touch, Colleen joined the conversation by announcing that she felt funny and proceeded to burp rather dramatically all over herself, Maureen, and the car.

Upon arriving home, the resident artists gave the tour of the kitchen's art work of finger paintings and homemade Valentines, our patron held the baby, Patrick played records, and Maureen and Colleen danced as I assembled the p, b, & j's for the younger customers and, in honor of my grand opening, a spinach salad for the more calorie conscious.

The grand opening day happened to coincide with the baby's doctor appointment. After lunch, my lucky guest participated in some invigorating postluncheon entertainment dressing four children in boots, mittens and coats to go outdoors. That done, we loaded them into the car, which wouldn't start. After numerous attempts, we gave up.

The six of us – me carrying the baby and the now-bewildered columnist carrying Maureen trudged through the snow to my neighbor's, who generously offered me the use of her car. After piling in once again we set off, dodging snow banks. We arrived at the doctor's office only to find a filled parking lot.

The role of chauffeur now switched. My little friends and I got out of the car as an even more befuddled journalist drove off searching for a parking place. Upon finding one he brought me the keys and hastily departed to a taxicab, which delivered him to – by comparison – the tranquil and sane *Washington Post* newsroom.

Epilogue

Allowing him a few recovery days, I queried Richard Cohen: "Could my kitchen make a go of it?"

"It has certain advantages," he replied. "It's safe – the only under-the-table activity would be kids looking for crayons. I like it even if the background music is unnerving."

With this glowing review I'm open for reservations.

March 8, 1979

. . . .

RICHARD COHEN
The Reason Why Women Work

THE MOMENT BUILT slowly. It came only after her daughter had thrown up in the car and the ride itself had not gone well, and when we arrived her older boy had played the phonograph at top volume and the other kids unwrapped a gift and shredded the wrapping paper over the living room rug, and then the older girl, sulking, disappeared for a time – gone, just gone – and the infant was given to me to hold while I ate my lunch with one free hand. It was then that the moment came.

She took the infant from me – this little thing, five weeks old with red hair like the other three kids – and she lifted her sweater and nursed the child. The other children were begging for attention, all of them snowbound, the older one, the boy, six years old and with the energy of a cooped fox, demanding to be heard, to be seen, to have his very presence acknowledged. It was then that I popped the question.

It is time to pause. Time to do what they do in the movies – a flashback. The lady's name is Kate Cavanaugh. She is 35 years old, red haired, the mother of four and the wife of John Cavanaugh, the congressman from the area around Omaha, NE. When her husband was first elected, Kate Cavanaugh was asked by an Omaha weekly paper to write a column about the glamorous life in Washington – caviar at the Iranian Embassy, balls at the White House, opening nights at the Kennedy Center. She consented, but a funny thing happened when she sat down to write. She had almost nothing glamorous to report. Instead, she was writing about the Washington supermarkets and the time a raccoon got stuck in her chimney, and what it feels like to turn 35. It's not that she never goes to the White House – she does – it's just that she doesn't go if she can't find a baby sitter. Nancy Kissinger did not have these problems.

Anyway, she called and she said that she had read about my having lunch with Art Buchwald, the famous and witty columnist who is seeking a new steady restaurant to replace the Sans Souci and she wanted to duplicate it. It would be lunch at her house, and the fare would be peanut butter and jelly sandwiches and would I do it? Yes, I would do it. I mean, I was charmed. She knew the column, and now she wanted the columnist to lunch. Of course I would come.

But on the day of the lunch my car was snowed in and so she had to come for me. She arrived with a car full of kids, all of them in the back, the infant in a portable crib, and about half a mile out, the eldest of the three girls threw up. She looked pale and car sick and mortified – after all, she is five – but she was comforted by her younger sister, another red-haired thing, perfect like on a cereal box.

When we got to the house, the older boy turned on the phonograph as loud as it would go, and the other kids wanted milk, and

Kate Cavanaugh complied. She walked around the kitchen with the infant on her hip or in her arms or sometimes she just handed it to me – here. I was this columnist – she clearly did not understand that – and not some participant, but I had this infant – God, what a cute kid – this infant with the lyrical Irish name of Machaela, and I sat at the table and tried to eat salad with one hand.

Kate Cavanaugh sat opposite me. All around the whole thing was coming apart – children going on little search-and-destroy missions in the kitchen. I watched and I listened and asked if she ever wanted to scream, and she said, "What do you mean 'want' – I do." I asked her if this ever gets to her and she said it does, and then I asked her why in the world she does it – mothering, housewifery.

She just stared at me. She looked at me as if I had asked her something offensive, something shocking or something so stupid she could not begin to understand what I meant. It was nothing like that, of course. She knew what I meant, knew probably that I and lots of others have this bias, look down on full-time, all-the-time mothers, uphold the wonderful value of "work," work-work, salaried work, out-of-home work like the type Jackie Kennedy does and Ms. Magazine wrote about – work for reasons other than money.

This is important now. You have to work for fulfillment, for the psychic pleasure of the thing, for self-satisfaction. This is what terrific people do, terrific women, of course, but terrific men, too.

One of the things you kept reading about Nelson Rockefeller was that he worked even though he didn't have to. This made him wonderful, a touch better than people who work because they have to. You get the feeling that if he had not worked, if he had just read books and just been wonderful to people, no one would have written his obituary – Nelson Rockefeller, reader of books and nice guy. Just the sound of it makes you want to laugh.

Kate Cavanaugh, the columnist, was nursing her baby when she answered my question – at least I think that's when she said it. "It's my job," she said simply. "I'm a mother."

Sometime later, Kate Cavanaugh found the time to write her column. I wrote three or four, and found some time to spend with my son. It's not as much as I want but I can't help it it's my job. I'm a columnist. THE WASHINGTON POST

March 1, 1979

Kate's Not Ready Yet To Be Age 35

One of my theories on life has been demolished. It was put to the supreme test and it failed miserably. What was the celebrated theory and what caused its failure?

The theory is about age, numerical age. I have asserted that it never bothered me. So far I have been able to accept gracefully each additional year. There seems to be redeeming qualities in every phase of life.

Shortly after my 30th birthday I had a philosophical discussion on age with Ted Reeder, who's slightly over 40. He said he was glad he wasn't 30 anymore, compared to what he knows and has experienced now, ten years later, he was very naive at thirty. I said I felt the same way about being twenty again. I had enjoyed that time. I relished every two-for-one beer at the Golden Buda and every verse of "Chicago" sung at Bill Bailey's Banjo Bar, but it was a time of restlessness. The mellowing which comes with an additional ten years has given me a feeling of contentment.

Seems like a logical theory, doesn't it? I thought so until March 1st when I brought my morning *Washington Post* into the house. If you will recall in my column previous to this, I related my experience with Richard Cohen, the Post columnist who came over to test out my kitchen as the new place to see and be seen. Well, he also did a column about our get-together which appeared March 1st. I knew that it would be in, we had discussed it over the phone. Naturally, looking for Richard Cohen's column was my first order of business that morning.

After quickly ruffling through the papers, my eye hit on his column which was entitled, "The Reason Why Women Work." I was delighted this very popular *Washington Post* columnist (who's also a father) was writing about me (a mother) who's also a columnist. As I rapidly scanned the article (with plans to reread each printed word) it happened. Right in the third paragraph: Kate Cavanaugh, 35. I was crestfallen. How could this happen – I'm not

35, I'm 31! There's a big difference there. I had to do something, but what? Hold the presses? Too late for that. It was 8 a.m. The doorsteps in Washington had received their Post at least an hour earlier. I decided to make the best of it.

It wasn't easy. According to my theory on age, being depicted as a 35-year-old shouldn't bother me, but it did – a lot. All of Washington thinks I'm four years older than I am. It's written in the paper – why shouldn't they believe it? I've never gone around telling people my age, or asking theirs. It seemed to be bad manners, but now I feel inclined to initiate every conversation with "I was born in the late forties," or "my older brother and my older sister helped my parents celebrate their 35th anniversary last month," especially if Richard Cohen's story is mentioned.

There's probably someone reading this who is 35 and who is thinking, "What's her problem? I'm 35 and it isn't that bad." Of course it's not if your 35 but I'm not and I'm not ready to be. I will be in four years.

After reflecting on Cohen's faux pax I realized what bothered me the most. At this point, at 31 years, I'm just where I want to be. I'm in the passage where I don't have time to read the book Passages. In four more years, however, my children who are six years and under will be ten years and under and I'll be in a different passage. Besides, according to Ted Reeder's philosophy, I'm not smart enough yet to be 35.

March 22, 1979

. . . .

Kate Has An Evening of Enchantment

John and I attended the state dinner held in honor of the signing of the Israel-Egyptian peace treaty. It was a tremendously historic occasion. All of official Washington was willing to stand out in the cold for a chance to dine at the White House and celebrate peace.

The dinner was the largest state occasion held in recent memory with 1300 invited guests. To accommodate the number, a huge tent filled with elegantly set tables was put up on the south lawn.

When we arrived at 7:15 a line leading to the White House had already formed. In the next few minutes it had extended all the way to Pennsylvania Avenue. The doors opened "promptly at 7:30" with the guards checking off the guests whose entry card was the telegram inviting them. As we waited in the near freezing temperatures, one guest commented about all "the power" shivering on the sidewalk. However, not even teeth chattering could put a chill on the evening. Everyone waited patiently to be admitted, including Lynda Johnson Robb who once called the White House home and several other notables who hope to do the same. Even Ted Kennedy, whose plans for a change in residence are still up in the air, took his place at the end of the line.

Upon arriving in the tent the excitement was almost overwhelming. The table hopping could be likened to a college prom or an Irish wedding. After the meal was served and before the official toast, most everyone was up and milling about. It was a night like no other and the crowd was making the most of it.

Within ten minutes I exchanged glances with Henry Kissinger, received a big kiss and hug from Tip O'Neill, kissed Miss Lillian and agreed with her that John is the cutest congressman, accepted congratulations on Machaela's birth from Vice President Mondale, congratulated and thanked President Carter for his success in making the treaty, glimpsed Prime Minister Begin who was already surrounded, and almost swooned when I shook hands with President Sadat.

With pounding heart and whirling head I returned to our table where we toasted the peace treaty with champagne and chocolate mousse. Shalom!

April 5, 1979

Patrick Sums Up Iran: 'A Big Mess'

I heard Patrick pouring the cereal into bowls and then I heard Colleen, as she put the English muffins into the toaster, tell her overnight guest, Alicia, to get the butter out of the refrigerator. It was a Saturday morning and our Saturday morning routine, which is the kids fend for themselves and I monitor the situation from my bedroom where I am lying with my ears open and my eyes closed, was in action.

Usually I listen to make sure no irreparable damage is being done to the kitchen or to them, but last Saturday I tuned into their conversation when I heard them talking about the Shah.

Patrick was telling the girls that the Shah was sick in New York but now he is feeling better and wants to leave the hospital but he doesn't have any place to go. He can't go back to Iran because everyone there is mad at him but they have all these Americans held as hostages until he comes back.

Then Patrick explained that the Shah used to be the boss of Iran but now the boss is a guy who wears a long coat and has a long beard. He has made everyone in the U.S. mad because he calls the president names and has all these people tied up.

As he poured milk on the cereal he summed it up, "It's a big mess."

As I listened to Patrick's view of current events, I realized he had some of the circumstances mixed up but he had one thing right, it is a big mess.

Iran is consuming our lives. It is making us angry and it is making us fearful. We are fearful for the well-being of the hostages, we are fearful of our country's positions in the world, and we are beginning to be fearful of losing our way of life, a peaceful life, a life we enjoy and have taken for granted.

At his news conference last week, President Carter said, "Every waking moment his thoughts are on the American hostages."

The American people have joined him in his vigil. Since the take-over of the Embassy in Tehran, I begin and end my day listening to world news. Every morning my radio alarm clock clicks on and I immediately focus on the news of what happened overnight.

As soon as I come downstairs, I go to the front door, get the newspaper, and before starting breakfast I rapidly read the lead stories hoping for some encouraging news.

John leaves for work, the kids go to school, Maureen, the baby, and I stay home but talk of "the crisis" surrounds the otherwise normal day. Phone conversations about car pools or plans for the evening inevitably stray to a discussion on the Ayatollah or the U.N. Security Council.

Our prayers at mealtime are no longer just a thanksgiving for our bountiful life but an urgent petition for the hostages well being and release.

At church in addition to the Advent hymns traditional at this time of the year, the congregation is singing the "Star Spangled Banner" and "America the Beautiful" as a sign of our support of the President and the U.S. policy.

I end the day by watching the nightly "Special News Report on Iran." Then I go to bed worried.

During my lifetime the United States has gone through many international crises. The Korean War happened when I was too young to remember, the Bay of Pigs happened when I was too naive to understand and when Vietnam came I was mixed up and confused. I just knew I didn't like it.

But Iran is different. No longer am I too young or too naive or too confused to remember and to understand. I know now why I don't like what is going on. But for the first time in my life the American people are drawn together with one purpose.

It is this spirit which will see us through the crisis. I pray for the resolution of the Embassy take-over so that this holiday season a truly United States can extol "Joy to the World," "Peace on earth and good will to men."

December 13, 1979

Kate Glances Back . . .
and Looks Ahead

In December, 1976, we were walking along East Capitol Street pushing our 7-week-old baby, Maureen, in the carriage. John stopped and looked up at the Capitol Building looming right in front of us all lit up and magnificently impressive. Then he turned and asked, "Do you think you will be happy here?"

"I don't know if I'll be able to stand the excitement," I replied.

We had been in Washington for about four days filled with rounds of meeting new people, festivities and seeing the nation's capital as a newcomer but also as an insider. I don't know when my heart stopped pounding.

I rode home from the Kennedy Center in a limousine with the newly-elected Speaker of the House, Tip O'Neill. I showed off my baby as I greeted the newly-elected Vice President, Fritz Mondale. He was raking leaves. I witnessed a historic race for the post of House Majority Leader within the Democratic Caucus.

In the three years since, the pace of events – or at least my participation in them – has slowed, but my enthusiasm for them hasn't. If John would ask me that same question today, I would be able to answer "yes."

Yes, I have been happy living in Washington. It is a great honor to be the wife of a member of the U.S. Congress; it is a wonderful experience, and it is also a lot of fun.

But my happiness didn't begin when John took his seat in Congress. I have always been happy, happy in our political life and happy in our marriage.

When I first met John it was 1968 and his dad was running for Congress, for the seat John holds now. It was an exciting time, a time of Bobby Kennedy and Gene McCarthy, a time when the country was so torn apart it was frightening to look to the future.

John introduced me to politics. He showed me that to get things done in this country you have to choose a person you can trust, one you can believe in. You find someone who understands our society and you work for him. That election day I worked at the polls giving out cards for Jack Cavanaugh. I wasn't even old enough to vote.

The next year we were married. Things weren't much better in the country. Richard Nixon was president, John was in the army and the war in Vietnam continued. Nevertheless, we were happy together.

In 1972 we lived in a little green house on 35th Avenue. I never liked the color of that house, but I grew to like the house itself and my neighbors who are good and friendly people. They all supported John when he ran for the Legislature from that district. I supported him, too, because he had all the qualities he told me four years before a representative should have.

That campaign was run sort of by the seat of our pants. John voted for himself in the primary and then went to take a law school final exam. We went campaigning door-to-door every day when I finished teaching school and John was done with his classes.

We addressed envelopes to voters at our dining room table, and were happy. Why wouldn't we be? We had each other, a new baby and a chance to make a difference in the country.

By 1976 that little green house was getting smaller. The rooms were filled by us, our three children and my sister. It was a time for adventure. Those qualities we discussed eight years before were shining in John. I would watch him late at night on the ETV legislative review and think my husband was the smartest, most reasonable man in the world.

Many people must have agreed with me, because all our old friends and many, many new ones worked very hard addressing envelopes, giving coffees, inviting John to speak at their organizational functions and talking to friends: all to get John elected to Congress. Achieving this success with the support of our friends was personally fulfilling.

Since that time John has been re-elected to Congress, and we have added another child to our family. We have had many wonderful experiences in Washington. We've witnessed the signing of the Middle East peace treaty. We attended the inauguration of President

Carter. We met the Pope and heard him speak. And I attended Hubert Humphrey's funeral at the Capitol Rotunda.

We have made many new and lasting friendships both in the Congress and in the Washington community. We have enjoyed the city itself.

The events of the past 10 years have strengthened the initial bonds of matrimony. We have been able to make each other happy. This ability is a gift which John and I are so very grateful to have received.

Now, after 10 years of marriage and five political campaigns (three of John's and two of his dad's), we are making a change. John still has all those important qualities and will always be my favorite candidate, but he is not seeking re-election.

We have been given four beautiful children whom we want to cherish and to nourish with our love, our understanding, our time and attention. In turn, we hope they will give us great joy and satisfaction throughout our lives.

I feel good about this decision. The concern, affection and understanding of our decision that all of our friends here in Nebraska have shown has deeply touched and overwhelmed us. It has helped us know that we did the right thing. And if we had the chance to do everything all over again would I want to? Absolutely!

January 10, 1980

· ·

People Make The Difference

The moving van came yesterday and loaded up our belongings, the children are in Wisconsin in the care of Grandma and Grandpa while I am here in Washington packing up and saying goodbye to a city and a life that I have loved and enjoyed.

Last night John and I had dinner at the White House. The President and Mrs. Carter invited us and the other retiring members of Congress for a farewell dinner. It was a wonderful evening, one that I will long remember. After it was over, we drove back to our neighbor's house where we spent the night.

I felt that last night summed up our time in Washington. We have many wonderful memories. Some of them are of dancing to Peter Duchin's orchestra at the White House Christmas Ball and others are of sitting on our patio laughing at a funny birthday card a neighbor and friend made for John.

I am going to miss it here. I feel somewhat like I did when I graduated from college. I had lived, laughed and cried (a lot the first year) all through those four years of school. When it was time for graduation it was very painful saying goodbye to that life. That doesn't mean I wanted my college years to continue, because I didn't. It was time for a change and I was anxious to see what was ahead.

I've come to the conclusion that change is difficult no matter how determinedly you seek it. If I were overjoyed at the prospect of leaving Washington it would mean that I hadn't been happy here, and I have been happy, very happy. Yet, I'm also excited about our return to Omaha.

We are sorry to leave our house here. After last evening's dinner at the White House, John and I stopped off at our empty house to pick up a few of our remaining things and to say goodbye. It was a sentimental visit. We relived our first night in the house; the excitement we felt at the prospect of making that house our Washington home. The barren living room and dining room reminded us of three years back when we didn't have any furniture but had plenty of space for all the guests at my surprise birthday party. We laughed as we talked of the changes we made in the house, one being the eviction of the raccoon from the attic.

More than our house we will miss the people who have become part of our lives. Our Maureen, whose every other sentence pertained to Amy Gray, will miss her inseparable friend, but eventually (and unfortunately) her memory of Amy will grow dimmer but it won't for me. I'll always have a very vivid picture of the two little girls sitting in the bath tub after Maureen cut Amy's hair.

My friend Mary Stanford is always helping me out. She says her children are somewhat grown up and mine aren't so I need the help. She tells me, "When you're 50 you can help out someone expecting her fifth child. Of course, it will probably be against the law to have five children then." I'll miss her because she says things like that.

Since John made this decision to leave Congress and we decided to return to Omaha, I have been asked many times what have been the highlights of our time here. I can answer that question two ways, either about our public life or about our private life.

Unquestionably our public life has been very exciting and I would find it difficult to pinpoint one highlight. We attended the state dinner celebrating the signing of the Middle East Peace Treaty, the funeral of Hubert Humphrey and the reception for Pope John Paul at the White House. I traveled with John to Belgrade, Yugoslavia for the International Monetary Fund Conference.

The high point of our private life has been the people who enriched our lives on a day-to-day basis. We have made friends we can count on and always enjoy. The friendships in the Congress, in our neighborhood and around the Washington area are genuine and long-lasting. That is reassuring because even though I am leaving Washington with a lump in my throat and an ache in my heart, I know the gap will be filled quickly as we resume our lives in Omaha. We found the old cliche, "It's the people who make the difference," applied in Washington. We've always known it applied in Omaha.

September 4, 1980

4 • BUMS LIVE HERE

Questions Reveal Compulsion to Clean House

Colleen had a conversation with her friends about what they do when they get depressed.

Kelly said she bakes something, Andrea said she goes shopping and Molly said she talks on the phone.

"What do you do when you get depressed, Mom?" Colleen asked.

"I clean . . . it seems like I get depressed when the house is a mess. If I get it cleaned, my mood improves dramatically."

Her assessment: "That's weird."

That may be, but it's a well-known fact around our house – ask anyone in the family – that my mood is directly related to the general appearance of our surroundings.

If the house is cleaned, my disposition is up, but if things are in disarray so am I, and everyone knows that they had better help clean up or, better yet, clear out.

I love to be left alone in the house so I can get things done. My idea of a good time is when John takes all the kids on an outing and I stay behind with the vacuum cleaner, the broom and a can of bathroom cleanser.

You probably think I'm kidding, but I'm not. I truly enjoy being alone and being able to make some order out of chaos and have it last, at least for a short time.

Although I'm not much for late-night socializing, I can burn the midnight oil dust-mopping under the couch and scouring the kitchen sink.

Don't I sound like fun? I could belong to Compulsive Cleaners Anonymous if there were such an organization, but the other members might blackball me as unfit, if they saw my house.

I can just hear the discourse among the other oven cleaners.

"She can't possibly have an excessive cleaning problem, because if she did her house wouldn't be such a mess all the time."

That baffles me, too.

A quiz to indicate "housecleanaholic" tendencies might include:

– Do you clean when you are alone?

– Do you clean when you should be doing something else like relaxing or sleeping?

– Do you clean three or more times a day?

– Do you make excuses to avoid social occasions so you can stay home and clean?

– When company arrives unexpectedly and you've been cleaning all day, do you act as if you've done nothing more than fluff the pillows on the sofa?

If you answer yes to most of these questions, which I did, then you also have reason to rein in the dust cloth and the Windex bottle.

It's comforting to know that I am not alone. In fact, housekeeping tasks consume so much of our (meaning Miss, Mrs. and Mr. America's) lives I'm convinced that if we eliminated from our speech all references to household chores there would be a sudden dearth of conversation.

Which would be great – if we could eliminate the messy house at the same time. Then we would have even more time to talk about something everyone is bound to be interested in – our kids!

May 14, 1986

Homes Hatch Plots to Spend Owners' Money

We got a new spring for the garage door! I know you are jealous because you've been dying to get a new spring for your garage door. To add to your envy, we also had three new clamps put on the door itself.

You're not jealous? You weren't coveting a new garage door spring? To be honest, neither was I until I couldn't get my garage door opened. To save a dollar, I wanted John to fix the spring so I could spend the dollar someplace more fun – at the grocery store, for example. But fixing garage doors is not one of his skills, so I called a repairman.

Homes are imaginative. They never cease to amaze me with the clever ways they think up to spend their owners' money.

Just when I think I've encountered every possible repair a house could need, I'm surprised with a before unthought-of problem, accompanied by an equally unanticipated bill.

This week it was the garage door spring. Last month, it was a burned-out pilot light on the water heater, which I discovered as I stepped into a cold shower.

Before that it was the rubber gasket that seals the clothes dryer door, the front door latch, the motor on the dishwasher, the heating element in the oven, the bearing in the furnace blower and the furnace thermostat.

I checked around to see how other houses were imaginatively spending their owners' money. One house told me that right after its owner settled in, it demanded a new foundation.

"I told the husband and wife that I wasn't about to hold up a bunch of rowdy kids unless they shored me up with some new mortar," the house said.

Another house gave me the lonely basement story.

"It was always dark down here. To get some attention, I began letting in a little water each time it rained. After a big storm I had a foot of water on my floor."

"Pretty soon there was a bunch of guys down here with jackhammers cutting up my floor trying to waterproof me. Boy, was I sore when they finished, and so were my owners when they got the bill."

The response to the question I posed to a few houses, "Do you celebrate holidays?" was overwhelming.

One house said, "I tell all my plumbing and appliances to relax and enjoy the holiday and try not to fizzle out, clog up or get jammed. But as most homeowners who pay double time for holiday repair charges know, there's always something."

The garbage disposal gets edgy after grinding up potato peels at Thanksgiving. The refrigerator breaks into a sweat when a watermelon and four six packs of beer are crammed around the potato salad on the Fourth of July. On Labor Day, the washing machine drain thinks it deserves a day off and backs up water on the laundry room floor.

One wise old Colonial offered this: "We houses often cause our owners unexpected inconvenience and expense, but many of our problems are resident inflicted. A video recorder I know told me the repairman discovered that it's malfunction was caused by a Susie Sea-Wee doll stuck in its cartridge holder."

Added his sage Victorian neighbor, "That's true, so be nice to us. After all we are the roof over your heads!"

"That's a fair request," I said. "If you promise to write the check when that roof starts leaking."

November 20, 1985

Not Only Cans Collect Garbage

We have four garbage cans. Three of them are brown and shaped like a cylinder, and the fourth is blue and shaped like a station wagon.

Appropriately, the car and cans sit next to each other in the garage, and I have to walk by one to get to the other.

The difference is, I walk to the trash can to put in trash. I don't put trash in the car – it's already there when I climb in.

Every week, we drag the trash cans out to the curb, and they are emptied into the garbage truck. It would be great if I could park the car at the end of the driveway, and when the trash collector came, he could pick up the car and shake all the junk into the garbage truck.

Why don't I just clean it out? I do, but it doesn't last. There is potential for a new mess every time we drive off.

What is all the junk, and why is it in the car? It's there because children carry belongings into the car but no one ever seems to carry anything from the car into the house.

Heck, if they did, it would spoil all the fun we have frantically searching the house for a book bag, the Brownie permission slip or the gym shoes that were forgotten in the car.

I'm not guilt free. I don't always take in all of my belongings either, but I feel I have an excuse: by the time I unload two car seats and carry in the occupants – who are usually asleep, until I lay them in their cribs – go back, unload the groceries and then take in the dry cleaning, I've forgotten about my purse, the cleaning coupons and the library books still on the car seat.

The children aren't as legitimately exempt. When we pull into the garage, they all jump out of the car – empty handed – before I can shift into park.

This forgetfulness extends to all riders in our car. Invariably, upon taking inventory of the accumulated car junk, I find things that belong to other people's children. Jackets, school papers and book bags are the most common abandoned items, but one week, Tom's terrarium, Hannah's dancing bag, Michelle's soap opera magazine and Andrea's school uniform were left behind.

Occasionally, when it becomes too embarrassing to be seen at a stoplight in such a junk-laden car, or when enough things are missing, or when I'm about to give a non-family member a ride, we clean it out.

I usually send someone out with a paper bag to collect the junk. If I feel industrious, I lug out the vacuum cleaner.

One day, Colleen started the job. After surveying her collection – two rain slickers, one ballet shoe, a notice about a confirmation meeting held two weeks ago, and a Cabbage Patch Doll's shoe whose loss we've already mourned – I decided to complete the chore myself.

Colleen said everything she left behind was too gross to touch.

I managed to garner another bag of treasures, some dating back to last summer's car trip to Wisconsin.

There were pieces from a Rainbow Brite Colorform set, flashcards of the "blend" sounds, and parts of a cardboard face mask from a fast food restaurant.

And that was just the surface junk. When I stuck my hand between the seat cushions, I was rewarded with handfuls of sticky candy, candy wrappers, lots of ink pens, barrettes, more Rainbow Brite colorforms and a pile of money totaling 51 cents.

The luxury foreign car is very much in vogue these days. I think I'd look real high falutin' driving around town in one.

But even if my budget could withstand such an expenditure, it wouldn't be a very practical purchase, which is too bad.

Since we're going to make a mess, it would be fun to do it in style.

May 29, 1985

Those Cereal Dishes Must Be 'Bulldozed'

At dinner the other night Patrick said, "In Spanish class today we learned that in Spain they eat five meals a day."

As we sat there in the midst of our third meal of the day, I thought, "I'm glad I don't have to prepare two more meals" but then I reconsidered and wondered, "How do they get away with only five meals?"

At our house we don't have three meals or five meals a day. We have one meal and it lasts all day long. This non-stop eating is a pain in the dishwater. My kitchen is either a mess, just recovering from a mess, or on its way to becoming a new mess.

Before I can start making a real meal, I have to run a bulldozer down the kitchen counter. If I'd wise up I'd just skip the meal – mainly because no one is interested in eating it anyway. It is too nutritious. I'm convinced our family gets together for the evening meal solely to spill glasses of milk.

Cereal is what everyone likes around here. They start out the day eating cereal and if I'd let them they'd pass the day eating cereal. Certain brands of cereal are more popular than others. The more sugary and junky the cereal, the faster it is eaten. We have two gallons of milk, one to pour on the cereal and one to pour on the floor whenever Captain Sugar Flakes are on special at the grocery store.

We've had some tearful scenes when the big kids get home from school and wipe out the good cereal supply that the little kids think should last forever – or at least until they've eaten their third or fourth bowl for the day. Usually, no alternative snack that I suggest such as "How about a carrot stick?" ever calms them down.

Sometimes if I'm lucky the fit is abated by offering broken up graham crackers with milk poured over them. Sometimes I think I could cut out all my decision-making in the grocery store and just buy graham crackers and milk.

I probably wouldn't save any money because I would have to buy so many boxes. We never eat more than half of what I buy. The other half gets dumped on the floor and then stepped on.

I have done something to save money. More than the cold cereals and the graham crackers, our family loves those individual servings of oatmeal, the ones which are packaged in envelopes and prepared by adding hot water. I rarely buy them, although they are good – good and expensive.

I hate spending so much money on something that vanishes so fast. Patrick's favorite after-school position is in front of the television hunched over his bowl of hot cereal, surrounded by numerous empty envelopes.

My new kick is to buy the comparatively inexpensive oatmeal in the round box, the kind with the meatloaf recipe on the label, and fix several servings at once in a pan on the stovetop. My breakfast clubbers can add their own brown sugar or cinnamon which they will overdo.

I'm so proud of myself when I cook this because it is one of those stick to the ribs breakfast. I know this because it sticks to the dishes. Once the cereal has dried to the bowl, it takes a jack hammer to get it off. Since I don't have a jack hammer I use a scouring pad and by the time I finish washing up it is lunch time.

"No problem," I say. "The bowls are clean; let those flakes pour!"

January 28, 1987

Kitchen Remodeling Cooks Up Chaos

Have you heard the saying that you should write what you know?

I have and all I know lately is that I'm cooking in the basement. We are getting a new kitchen.

We were evicted from the old kitchen a couple weeks ago, and ever since we have been living on tuna fish sandwiches and Girl Scout cookies.

Before the old kitchen went to pot and pan heaven, I planned how I would cope while the work was being done. I thought it wouldn't be any hardship at all not having a kitchen for a while because I have a partial kitchen in the basement which includes cabinets, a two-burner hot plate, a sink and a refrigerator.

I could bring down my microwave and toaster oven and we'd have easy eating. What I hadn't counted on was:

– The counters being filled with paint cans and screw drivers;

– The ceiling and cabinet shelves being torn out to do the plumbing work above,

– More junk than I will ever need loaded in boxes and sitting all over the place;

– The table I had planned to use for meals covered with tools and clay pots of last summer's geraniums. I could clear off the table but I've never gotten around to it.

So how are things working out? We have been eating out or carrying in, or grabbing whatever can be found. Occasionally, I've made a complete meal.

Since fast food gets expensive, I've been scrounging coupons and restaurant specials. But taking this gang to a restaurant is an ordeal for me as well as for the restaurateur, so I try not to do it frequently.

Instead, most evenings I think about cooking something but get so overwhelmed at the prospect that I seek out a can opener and begin opening cans of ravioli, whole cranberry sauce, and sliced mushrooms.

One evening we made a meal of four cans of pop-open rolls baked in the toaster oven. I didn't think we needed 40 rolls but everyone wanted a chance to pop a tube.

On a few occasions I've made a real meal such as the three-fourths cooked chicken I fixed in the microwave and broiled in the toaster oven and the Swiss steak I thought was delicious. We carried the meals upstairs, pushed the refrigerator out of the way, dusted the saw dust off the chairs, and sat down to eat at the family table. But most of the time we sit wherever we can.

Usually, I tell the little kids to sit on one basement step and use the step above them as a table. The rest of us either stand or perch on a pile of ceiling tiles or a roll of insulation.

I know that when the new kitchen is all done it will be wonderful. That is, if it happens before I'm all done in.

March 25, 1987

Bill System Delays Day of Reckoning

It is the first of the month again, which means it is time to pay bills.

Of course, I probably won't get around to paying them until the 13th or 14th despite my desire to quickly get over this nasty business.

If I were more organized and had an uninterrupted cash flow, I might be able to satisfy my creditors long before they feel obligated to send me their polite "Did you forget?" query, qualified with the timid statement, "If your payment is in the mail, thank you and please disregard this notice." But my lack of excess order is topped only by my lack of excess money.

I wish I could get my bills paid right away each month, because I'd feel so relieved. I hate having that obligation hanging over my head like a storm cloud.

At the outset of the month I begin telling myself, "Today is the day I'm going to sit down and settle my accounts." However, something always comes up, like a chance to go somewhere and spend more money, which prevents me from becoming fiscally responsible.

I have a system for taking care of my finances. I judge the system to be successful because since I've been using it I haven't been put in jail for delinquency and the chance that I will be arrested in the future looks dim. This is how it works. I have a basket in which I put all the bills, letters to be answered and papers to be filed. Once a month I bring it out to sort everything. My intention is to eventually end up with an empty basket.

Before I can tackle this problem I have to balance my checkbook. This can take time. I know you are supposed to write down and subtract the checks as they are written, but I like to live dangerously.

Anyway, after I settle my accounts I have to stare at the balance and then shake my head in disbelief at the amount of money I have already spent during the month. Usually this information is so discouraging that I decide I've had enough financial disclosures for one day.

Sometimes I get back to my bills the next day and sometimes it's the next week. When I do get around to it, I make a long list of my creditors and next to each name I write the amount I owe, then I total it up.

The moment of reckoning finally arrives. Who gets paid the maximum amount? Who gets only the minimum due? Who gets something in between? And who gets slighted until next month?

You may be thinking this isn't the most sensible approach for handling finances – as all those creditors tell me, "your credit rating is your best asset."

But I don't have anything to worry about – my credit standing is in wonderful shape and I have evidence to prove it.

Every day I receive come-ons from companies offering me credit cards because of my excellent standing. John thinks this is pretty funny. He says those banks and department stores wouldn't be so quick to place an easy line of credit in my pocket if they realized the Ms. K. Cavanaugh whose business they so aggressively seek is the same person who puts Mrs. John Cavanaugh's credit in jeopardy.

Luckily for me the computers can add and subtract but can't put two and two together.

October 1, 1986

· ·

From Tiny Samples, Big Decisions Grow

Many times in life, you have to make a hard decision. The kind there's no turning back on, one of those "you made your bed, now lie or lay (or whatever is grammatically correct) in it" sort of decisions.

I have recently been struggling with one of those decisions. I can't go so far as to say it has been a real crisis of faith, because you'd probably think I'm being silly but it is close behind in the brain wracking, hemming and hawing department.

It is something equivalent to deciding on getting married or going to the World Series or opting to join the Foreign Legion or becoming a Lego Block assembler: We are painting our house and I decided to change the color.

Before you burst out giggling, think about it.

The color of your house is something you have to live with for a long time – at least, as long as the paint job lasts, which most folks hope is a very long time unless they've got a paint disaster fund stashed in an empty can of turpentine.

Every time you drive in the driveway, the house color stares you right in the eye. Every time you go outside for the newspaper even if you keep your head down fixed on the headlines of the day, your eye is bound to catch sight of a gutter, shutter, or garage door.

More importantly, every car pool that drives in the driveway, every friend that comes over, and every census taker, religious crusader, and miracle cleaning solution salesman that comes to the door will be eyeballing the color of your house – especially if it is the wrong color.

That is why it is a big decision to pick out the right color. I'd been camping out in the front yard with my back to the street, staring at the house. While the preparation work was in progress I stood holding various paint samples trying to visualize how each of the 1 inch by 3/4 inch paint chips would look multiplied 2000 times and spread across the front of the house. I've had all my friends, relatives, neighbors and anyone else that happened to be passing by give me an opinion.

I'm past that part now. The paint is on the house and it is so far so good. I like it.

Now I'm working on the shutter color. After an all-neighborhood pow wow I think I've decided to stick with my original plan, but I may still have to do a little experimenting by painting some old boards the different choices and putting them up against the house to see what color I like best.

Finally, I have to make one of those last but not least decisions. I've been hankering for a colorful front door. Whenever I see a house with one, I covet it; so I decided when I repainted my house I was going to have a door that makes a statement, that says something about who lives here.

Now that the door color picking time is here, I'm not sure what to do. Once again I've been resorting to the neighborhood opinion. I figure in a way they are entitled to a say because they also have to look at it.

Everyone says "Go for It. You want the house to be you and it won't be you unless it's a bit wacky and wild." I wonder what they mean by that remark.

Anyway, after that advice I've been experimenting. Today I found a bed sheet close to a color I'm considering. I hung it up over the door and then I walked out to the curb for a good look.

I liked what I saw. I wonder if my painter will mind carrying the sheet to the paint store to get the right color mixed.

My next decision is to decide what color ribbons to use on my Christmas wreath so it doesn't clash with my colored door. Now do you believe me that this isn't an easy project?

July 13, 1988

Kids' Lazy Days of Summer Can Drive a Mother Crazy

The song, "Those lazy, hazy, crazy days of summer . . . " keeps running through my head. I feel like it was written with me in mind, because on these hazy days my kids are lazy, and it's driving me crazy.

If they'd only do what I tell them, things would run so smoothly.

Patrick is by far the worst. I signed him up for a summer school class at (according to him) "the crack of dawn." It is at 9 a.m.

My motivation was to get him out of bed in the morning, otherwise he'd sleep well into the afternoon. Then I'd find myself plotting ways to get him up – lighting fireworks around the bed or turning the garden hose on him.

The younger family members, who I wish would sleep until noon, have no trouble getting up. But they transfer their pajama-clad bodies from the bed to the couch where they live out the rest of the morning watching television.

This ritual really gets to me, because it involves a whole new mess of blankets, pillows and cereal bowls with milk spilling out.

I put up with it for a little while, then lower the boom. Usually no one notices, until I up the volume and intensify my orders to, "Turn that thing off, pick up your junk, get dressed and make your bed."

Eventually we get this much accomplished, then I begin issuing the orders of the day.

Once again, everyone is oblivious. The other day I repeated myself so many times that finally I said, "I'm getting exhausted from having to yell so much." And Patrick said, "Well, don't yell."

"But no one does what I tell them to do unless I yell," I answered.

In hopes of eliminating some confrontations each day, I have been making lists of things that need doing. It seems so simple on paper. The jobs aren't particularly overwhelming. The older kids are to do such things as load the dishwasher, and the little ones are assigned such tasks as picking up papers in the yard. If everyone would cheerfully collect the lists and merrily go about performing their duties each day, we'd have a very serene, well-run home.

Don't laugh! I'm no dummy – I know it will never happen, but I have to keep trying.

Patrick thinks my lists are real dumb. Maureen and Machaela usually start doing the assigned jobs, but give them up halfway through. Johnny and Mike say the list is too hard, and baby Pete is too busy generating new household tasks to do any work.

Colleen is the only one to use her list. She thinks of it as her ticket out of here. When she asks if she can go somewhere, I say, "Yes, when the work is finished."

"It's never finished," is her reply, but she figures if she does what's on her list, she can go. I try to persuade her to stay by suggesting she invite her friends over to our house.

"They don't want to come over here," she says. "You always put them to work."

I don't look at it that way. I think I'm affording Colleen and her friends an opportunity for social interaction at the kitchen sink.

Patrick and Colleen tell me there's another side to my tale of woe.

"You are always making us work, and if we're not working, we are baby-sitting."

"We never get off duty. I can't go anywhere without some little kid hanging on me," Patrick says.

"Every time I go up to my room to read – you say reading is important – you think of something for me to do," Colleen adds. (Reading is important, but she's talking on the telephone).

So who are you going to believe?

Maybe the best attitude to adopt would be to sing the other song, "Summertime, and the living is easy," and wait until school starts again to clean up around here.

June 25, 1986

This Old Pan Is Chock-Full of Memories

The Dutch oven kettle was tough to get clean.

I had filled it with detergent and water in hopes of simplifying the task. Now I was hard at work scouring its bottom and sides, trying to remove the remnants of the split pea soup prepared by my sister Sheila, who was visiting from suburban Chicago with her husband and son.

As I worked I smiled to myself about the soup and the comments exchanged over dinner by Sheila and some ungrateful diners.

I ate the soup – I'll eat anything – but the others were not as enthusiastic. Sheila conceded that maybe next time she shouldn't make it while watching the Chicago Bears on television.

As I got a spatula to chip away the burned stuff stuck to the bottom of the pan, I wondered whether I would ever get it clean enough to use again. But then I remembered that this pan has undergone sandblasting like this many times before.

It has traveled around the stove's burners a time or two and has found itself undergoing grueling restoration therapy an equal number of times in my kitchen sink.

I've changed sinks several times but I've never changed my pans. I got them for a shower gift before my wedding.

In that pan there are nineteen years of boiling spaghetti and potatoes, hard cooking eggs for Easter, simmering stew to take to a grieving family when they've lost a loved one or to a rejoicing home when a new baby arrives.

That pan has held cookie batter at Christmas, as well as hand washables rinsed out in the kitchen sink – so they would not drip on the floor as they are carried to the clothesline.

Even the top of the pan has memories. The top suffers from the loss of the top pull. When I want to check what I'm cooking I lift up the edge of the pot's top with the handiest kitchen implement. A few years ago my Dad fashioned a wire pull for the top. That was wonderful, but it has since broken off.

During one Sunday dinner dishwashing session several years back, my husband's family accused my sister, Mary Pat, and me of speaking inaccurately when we called the pan's top a top. They said it should be called a lid. They said our misspeaking was a regional expression from Illinois (where we were from) but was still incorrect.

It turns out we both were wrong. Twelve years after that discussion, I decided to check it out by looking up an advertisement for cookware. It refers to tops or lids as tight fitting covers.

There are memories all around me, and one is a surprise every time my good china comes out for a special occasion.

An alarmed helper will ask me, "Kate, did you know this plate is broken?" When I answer, "Yes, that was broken before Colleen was born." Generally the next question is, "Why do you still have it?"

I still have it because it reminds me of the Christmas right before Colleen's birth. Gasoline wasn't sold on Sunday that winter so Barbara, another sister, and her husband, Bill stayed over with us until Monday, which was Christmas Eve, enroute home to Illinois from Kansas.

After we cooked breakfast, my very old sink got clogged and while we tried to free the waterway, the corroded pipe gave way. The result would have been no kitchen sink to prepare the Christmas Eve dinner but nothing like that was going to diminish our holiday plans.

We stuck a bucket underneath the sink and washed dishes in a kettle (I think it was my Dutch oven) and proceeded as scheduled. All was fine until after dinner, when the faucet which was also old fell into the dishwater breaking the china plate. If I had disposed of the plate I might not have remembered this episode.

The things that surround me hold memories because they have been a part of my life; not just for doing the jobs they were designed to do, but for doing their jobs at times and with people who mean a lot to me.

I like hanging on to the memories these things stir, so I'll be hanging on to my broken plate and Dutch oven. We can age gracefully together.

November 16, 1988

Do-It-Yourselfer Plumbs the Mysteries of Clogged Pipes

I'm waiting for the plumber to come.

I hated to call him. I wanted to fix the problem myself – not just to save the cost of a service call, although that would be nice – but because I have a fascination for plumbing.

I think what goes on between the walls, beneath the drains and under those sinks is fascinating and mysterious and I want to know all about it.

I like to be in harmony with my plumbing fixtures. I am sensitive to their moods and ons and offs. If a shower is being taken, I hear it. If dishes are being washed, I know it, mostly because I'm the only one who ever does them.

Croy

And if the water is running in the toilet in the basement two floors below, I can't sleep until I go all the way down there and stick a spatula or flyswatter in the tank to cut off the water supply.

One of the most exciting parts of our recent remodeling project was when the basement floor was jack hammered – well, that wasn't exciting, just noisy. I liked it when they put in the big pipes and connected them to other big pipes, "So," I thought, "that is where it all goes."

Over my homeowner years I have encountered a number of plumbing problems. At the beginning of this tour of duty I knew nothing about plumbing and now I've advanced to knowing next to nothing, but I feel like I know everything.

The first lesson at my first house was given to me by my neighbor.

I was completely intrigued when my bathroom sink was clogged and she explained how she knew the blockage was above the basement drain because the washing machine still drained out.

As exciting as that bit of knowledge was, it didn't give me quite the rush I had when my brother unclogged a bathroom sink at my second house.

This procedure was the work of a genius. He took the garden hose, stuck it through the bathroom window and placed it in the drain pipe opening he made by taking off the joint under the sink. The next step was to place a washcloth around the hose so the pressure could build up when the hose was turned on full steam.

This sudden surge of water caused whatever was lodged in the pipes to blast out, leaving me a free flowing drain.

I loved this and I wanted to try it out myself. I was delighted one day when a friend, after hearing of my slick unclogging method, asked me if I could do it for her.

Her husband arrived home as my friend was trying to toss the hose up to me as I hung out the second story bathroom window. To my amazement he didn't tell me thanks but "No thanks, we'll call a plumber."

Apparently, he trusted me because he began to assist me as I removed the "U" joint. All went well until I had to reassemble the pipe and I couldn't get it tight enough. My friends didn't think they could live with a bucket under the sink to catch the leaking water.

I had another plumbing challenge when a skewer from the Thanksgiving turkey got stuck in the disposal. That doesn't sound too tricky, does it?

I didn't think so either, but after struggling with it for three days I decided to detach the disposal and the skewer would slip right out. I think this might have worked if I hadn't been eight months pregnant and could have maneuvered under the sink.

After reading the Better Homes and Gardens home maintenance book, I thought I could install a new toilet. When we needed one I went out and purchased the new commode, brought it home and got to work.

When things were not fitting into place, I called my Dad long distance and spent more than I was saving on plumber's bills to receive his instructions and suggestions that I needed professional plumbing help.

After reviewing all these watery adventures I think I made the right decision today to call a plumber, but I think I'll hang around just in case he needs any help, advice or a garden hose.

November 11, 1987

Baskets Brim with the 'Stuff' That Homes Are Made Of

When we remodeled our kitchen last winter, one idea I had was to have a couple shelves in a built-in pantry for "my stuff."

I wanted a place where I could stuff this stuff as it accumulated, and then go through it when I had a few moments. Then I'd never have a messy counter, and my sleek new kitchen would be just that: sleek.

Has it worked? How well do you know me? To be fair to myself, it has sort of worked. I do gather the papers in neat piles. Sometimes I even go through them first. Then I put things away such as book bags, my purse, shoes and the rest of the "stuff" I put into a basket.

Croy

The basket is the problem. It is filled to capacity with stuff that has no home, yet I can't throw any of it away.

Telling you about this basket has inspired me to clean it out.

Sitting in front of me I have: clothes pins, the combination to a padlock, a small license plate with Mike's name on it, a bottle of fingernail hardener, a Brownie patch, football and baseball cards, a necklace wrapped around a gobot toy, a leg of a Silverhawk, a Barbie and the Rockers cassette tape, my garage door opener – I had been wondering where that was – a My Little Pony figure, and a My Little Pony pin, a Christmas tree cookie cutter, a Barbie boot, several Hot Wheels cars, crayons, a corn on the cob holder, Lego blocks (they are everywhere), a book of stamps, hair curlers and hair bows, the knob from a cabinet (which one I don't know) and the Snoopy pencil sharpener.

This kind of accumulation drives me nuts, but I don't know what to do about it. It seems like it is everywhere.

I have similar baskets in the laundry room and my bathroom. The kids would have one in their rooms if the rooms were picked up. They just have their homeless paraphernalia strewn about the floor.

This discussion prompted me to go on a mission to remedy this collection problem and I ended up at the dresser in my bedroom. I can't believe it.

Yesterday, the bureau top was cleaned off with just the pretty little knickknacks, jewelry boxes and pictures arranged nicely, but today it looks like I am getting ready for a white elephant sale. Slopped across the dresser top are two rolls of Scotch tape which is amazing because if I needed to use tape I wouldn't be able to find any.

There is also thread, He-Man's arm, a Little Kitty barrette, a dried bagel, cleaner's tags, eye shadow, an overdue library book notice, No. 15 sunscreen, matches, political buttons, two decks of cards, and two pairs of scissors.

In addition to all these baskets of valuables we have what is known as "the kitchen drawer." That is the first place you look if you are searching for anything.

We have approximately 20 drawers in our kitchen but only one "kitchen drawer." It is supposed to be the place for the phone book, but that took up the space needed for the hairbrushes, address books, keys for cars we no longer own, screw drivers, cleaning coupons, birthday candles, old batteries (and even some new ones), a coupon for Diet Coke (I could use that) and a scrap of paper with "swollen glands, headache" and the doctor's phone number written on it.

This overwhelming assortment of useless but indispensable goods is beginning to depress me. Maybe I better go out shopping for some new "stuff" and forget about it.

October 21, 1987

5 • JUNK IS A FOOD GROUP

Horan

Girl Scout Cookies Scattered Over House By Kids Taking a Bite Out of the Profits

We have two Brownies at our house who took orders for Girl Scout cookies several weeks ago.

Neither of them sold much door-to-door. I think they thought, "Why should we peddle cookies around the neighborhood when we have a customer at home (meaning me) who will buy enough for us to make a respectable showing?"

When I hear of the total number of boxes sold by other girls, I think, "Gee, we should have tried harder."

Other Brownies sell cookies to Mom's bowling team, Dad's entire work staff, Grandma's card club and every neighbor within a 2-mile radius. Their order forms look impressive when handed to the Brownie leader, especially next to the scantily marked order sheets from Maureen and Machaela.

This thought continues when it's time to pick up the orders and another Brownie is there with her mother, who is driving a borrowed half-ton truck to haul all the orders away.

However, all this guilt rapidly disappears when we get the cookies home. Not because I don't have to devote my weekend to sorting cookies, retracing the sales route, counting money and making change for a $5 bill. I'm relieved the girls didn't sell many cookies because they do an even poorer job of delivering them.

Before they get around to exchanging cookies for money with their limited clientele, their little brothers have opened the boxes, which means I end up opening my wallet.

The temptation is too great for the boys not to open as many boxes as they can get their hands on, take bites out of half the cookies and throw the rest around the room.

You could tour our house and sample the complete Girl Scout cookie line. In the entryway we have a crunched box of Golden Yangles. Sitting atop the washing machine is a paper tube of

Coconut Cremes. Scot-Teas can be found on Johnny and Mike's dresser. Chocollage cookies are broken into pieces on my closet floor. They are my favorite, but I didn't put them there.

One-year-old Pete was seen in the family room juggling the entire contents of a box of Hoedowns. He was offended when I took them away.

Thin Mints adorn the dining room table, and Thin-Mint fingerprints decorate the dining room walls. The peanut butter filling of Savannahs is smeared on the basement carpeting.

This arrangement does not sound very appetizing, does it? That's what the kids think, too. After wrecking one box of cookies, they feel compelled to open another.

"Too gross to eat," they say about the broken pieces of cookies. Too bad I don't think that way.

Each day of the Girl Scout cookie season, my calorie count escalates to a five-digit number. I wonder if I should write Girl Scout headquarters to suggest a warning label for each box that is a twist on the "be prepared" Scout motto: "Warning: Be prepared to gain weight."

A better idea would be for the Girl Scouts to get out of the cookie business and begin selling cans of spinach or lima beans. That wouldn't be as lucrative for the Scouts, but a lot of my problems would be solved.

March 19, 1986

....

Who Are The Wise Guys Labeling Cereal 'Free Inside'?

Is there someone that you'd like to punch out?

The potential recipients of my fist (although, none of them is ducking for cover) are the creators of breakfast cereal packaging.

I'm pretty fed up, and it is not because I've eaten too much Raisin Bran or Rice Chex.

Why don't they just pour the cereal into a box, put the name on it and send it off to the store? I know why and I can't quarrel with the cereal makers' attempt to make a profit, but I find fault with how they go at it.

My kids decide what cereal to get, not by how the cereal tastes but by what is "free inside." These were the first words our friend Mark John learned to read.

We, the cereal eaters of America, are paying $2 to $3 for colored cardboard toys worth 2 to 3 cents, which are surrounded by more colored cardboardlike pieces that are the cereal.

Not to be unfair to what I call the junk cereals, even the "healthy" ones do it, but their comeons are geared to the older eater. They offer picnic equipment, tennis shoes, roses, milk, travel discounts, and panty hose. None are "free inside" in case you are having a hard time visualizing the shape of the boxes. They are offers which have to sent for.

I made a gimmick-finding trip down the cereal aisle (By the way, I made this trip without my under-age shopping companions. Otherwise, I would have arrived home with the cereals instead of just a list of cereals. If you are thinking I don't have control over my children, you're right.) I discovered that:

For $3.33 you can get cereal plus a coupon for a free Blizzard. When you get home from the store with this great deal, your kids start bugging you until you give in and drive to the Dairy Queen which isn't close by and spend another $7 so everyone can have a Blizzard.

For $3.19 you can get Trix bubble gum, but as soon as you get home you'll need to pour out the cereal to find it. The kitchen counter or floor is a good place to do this.

How about the Garfield padlock? It comes unassembled. Do Fred Flintstone 3-D glasses interest you? They were good for a 3 dimensional fight between John, Mike, and Pete over who got to wear them first.

Glow-in-the-dark things are a real item, and so are monsters. The last time my guys were doing their grocery store begging, they told me how much they wanted the Crunch Cruiser, a silver-dollar-sized plastic Frisbee thing.

Once home, the kids dug through the box for it. The coveted item is never on top, so the search involves sticking your hands way down in the box, or holding it up and shifting the cereal contents to one side so you can see the bottom of the box, then sticking your hand in and retrieving it.

No one will eat the cereal now because it is all icky, but that doesn't matter because they only wanted what was "free inside." John and Mike went into the bathroom and turned out the lights, because the Crunch cruiser glowed in the dark, and tossed it back and forth and on the floor, where it stayed until later that day when I stepped on it. I put the crushed Crunch cruiser in the trash and so far no one has noticed.

We have also had free Skittles, SweetTarts candies, and we've made a complete set of boats, cars, and school rooms out of the Honeycomb boxes. We've sent for free water monsters with three price code symbols, and it only cost me $7.83 in cereal purchases.

In the future we have the opportunity to get Carefree gum, a Snickers Bar, a Wacky Whipper, gumballs, a checkers game, bubble gum, a flashlight, a Smurf chase game, a 3-D viewer, a whistle pop, 15 sets of baseball cards, a Nerds bike cap, Milky Way bar, pinball game, bike license plate, a baseball trivia book, and a free mask, which says "Attention Moms!" by its instructions.

But the most exciting possibility is the glow-in-the dark prehistoric tracks. I think I'll buy out the store for those and lay them all around the house of the guy who thinks up these things.

August 19, 1987

. . . .

No Fuss, No Mess Goals In Choosing Fast Foods

Occasionally we have fast food at our house. I like fast food, because it is fast, but I have other reasons for having a meal other than one I can fix in my kitchen.

Taste and nutrition are not even considered when making the fast-food selection. What I consider most is ease in cleanup.

I almost always veto the Colonel's chicken dinner because we have to put the mashed potatoes on plates and eat them with silverware. Pizza is my favorite choice because all we need are paper napkins or paper towels.

My next choice is the Golden Arches or the "Have It Your Way" place. The floor needs a good sweeping when the burger-and-fries meal is devoured or demolished, but otherwise the cleanup is easy. Everything can be eaten with fingers and the empty containers tossed out.

My problem arises when it is time to make the order.

Usually I ask everyone what they want to eat, which sounds easy, but I never order what they want.

They ask for food I consider either too expensive or unnecessary. Or they ask for an item they'll never eat, but they want it just because they've seen it advertised on television.

So I have to decide what to get, and I never make the right choice. I always get too many french fries and not enough cheeseburgers, or too many cheeseburgers and everyone wants a hamburger, and they won't eat the cheeseburgers even if I remove the cheese.

Why don't I just take everyone along and eat at the fast-food place? That way the mess would be the restaurant's to clean up.

Sometimes we do it that way, but I prefer not to, because if we eat "in" then we have to buy something to drink to go with the bits of chicken, hamburger or taco.

Of course, my kids don't want the drink. They like to have the drink to drop on the table and cry over, as it seeps into the french fries.

Usually an all-out lobbying campaign is launched to get a milkshake. My first response is, "No milkshake, not this time."

After repeated pleas, I give in and say, "OK, we'll get one but you have to share it." When that solution is deemed unsatisfactory, I cave in and everyone gets one except me. I finish the milkshakes that the loudest insisters are never able to.

If I'm thinking about getting dinner for the family at a fast-food restaurant, I hesitate at first over spending the money. I always say to myself, "It would be a lot cheaper if we fixed something at home."

So I use these arguments on myself: "I don't have anything thawed out to cook." "I'd have to go to the grocery store before I can cook anything." Or, "I just don't feel like making dinner."

I justify the expense as my only choice for feeding my hungry family, who thinks there's nothing more delicious than a meal attainable by ordering over the telephone, requesting it at a counter, or by getting one that mysteriously appears after we talk into a speaker box outside our car window.

As you may have guessed, I'm an easy mark for the fast-food line. But for reasons I can only blame on my upbringing, we never have carryout food on Sunday, with the exception of doughnuts after church.

Sunday is the day of rib roast, mashed potatoes and green beans – which is another way to say a home-cooked meal. It doesn't matter whose home it is cooked in, just as long as it isn't served out of a paper bag.

And we never have fast food two days in a row – unless we are getting work done on the house and we can't get into the kitchen, the electricity is off, the girls had dancing lessons, Patrick has a lot of homework, I have a lot of laundry, the lawn needs mowing, the car needs washing, John's out of town, John just got back into town or the weather is threatening.

We had Chinese takeout last night. I wonder if I can apply any of those exceptions to today's events and order a pizza for tonight?

May 28, 1986

Boxed Macaroni, Cheese Is Their Gourmet Delight

"What's for dinner?" Machaela asked when she ran into the kitchen looking for something to eat.

When I described the meal I was preparing, she moaned.

"Why don't we ever have anything good?"

"This will be good." I said about the chicken breasts, broccoli, baked potatoes and green salad I was preparing.

"Just grown-ups like that kind of stuff." she replied.

"Well, last night didn't we have something you liked – pork chops, apple sauce, au-gratin potatoes, and green beans?"

"Sort of. I liked the apple sauce."

"And what about the night before, when I made broiled sole, boiled new potatoes, and sauteed zucchini." I asked, feeling very domestic about cooking three real evening meals in a row.

"Are you making a joke? The only part I liked about that meal was squeezing the lemon over the fish. How come we never have spaghetti?" she asked. "The kind that comes in a can."

I could say we don't have a decent can opener. But that isn't the reason we don't have canned spaghetti. I have to eat these meals, too, and although I'm not a picky eater, if I have a choice I wouldn't choose what Machaela considers "good."

But when the mom and dad go out, the siblings are elated to fix canned spaghetti, ravioli, or boxed macaroni and cheese.

This last entree baffles me. They love it. I think I could buy it by the case and cook it by the barrelful.

But whenever I fix this, I feel a twinge of guilt for taking such a simple route for dinner, and a tremendous temptation to toss the box into the boiling water along with the macaroni. Once the box was boiled, drained and sprinkled with the envelope of so called cheese it would be hard to differentiate it from the macaroni.

The children of a mom I know were excited to hear they were having macaroni and cheese for dinner. This mom boiled macaroni, then she grated cheese, combined it with milk and butter. By stirring continuously over a double boiler she made a thick and rich sauce. She assembled the casserole, topped it with buttered bread crumbs and put it into the oven.

When it was ready, she called her family to the table and presented her dish. It would not do much to lower the cholesterol count but would appeal to most taste buds.

"What's this stuff?" they asked.

"Macaroni and cheese." The Mom answered. "No it's not," they said. "The noodles are too big and the cheese tastes too real. Macaroni and cheese comes out of a box."

She got a big box of sugared cereal and poured each kid a bowlful. They were delighted, and then she and her husband abandoned worries of clogged arteries and wolfed down the whole casserole.

The real problem with these young taste buds is that they are fickle. Most of the food they consider "Good" cost more than food that really is good, or at least good for you. But if I decide to have something that is good and expensive, suddenly they are gourmets.

For a Friday in Lent I decided to fix scallops, which was not exactly a meatless sacrifice except for my pocketbook. I figured I could manage the tab because my young eaters would turn up their noses at the costly seafood.

I was wrong. They all loved the scallops, and although I attempted a loaves and fishes scenario I still didn't have enough. Next time I'm getting out the macaroni and cheese first.

March 16, 1988

Good Food Travels Fast

The food was really good at the luncheon I had the other day. I could tell because it was the topic of conversation.

I can say this without sounding boastful because it was a group effort, with several people fixing various courses. My job was to get my house in presentable shape. Believe me, that is no simple job, but another column already told you all about that problem.

We set the food out buffet-style and once everyone helped themselves and sat down to eat, the raving began.

"Who made this?" one of the gals asked.

"It's delicious," another added. "I'm trying to figure out what is in it."

When the creator of that course listed the ingredients several ohs and ahs and several questions were heard.

"Oh, I wondered what gave it that spiciness!"

"Do you grate your own parmesean cheese or do you use the kind from the can?"

"Can I have the recipe?"

"This gelatin mold is beautiful. It looks too pretty to cut into," was a comment made as the eaters progressed through the buffet line. The hesitation at performing Jell-o surgery quickly passed and everyone helped themselves.

"What gives this such an unusual texture?" someone asked the Jell-o lady.

"What do you do to make those beautiful garnishes," another asked.

"Can I have that recipe?"

The next conversation heard all over the room concerned the rolls.

"These rolls smell so good and taste even better. I bet they are impossible to make."

"They aren't too tough to do," the baker said.

"Can I have the recipe?"

Finally there was a lull in the discussion of food preparation as everyone discussed how they had eaten way too much. After an interim long enough to clean away the plates, desserts were served.

These irresistible desserts, which no one had room for or thought they should eat, were consumed with great relish. Between bites you could hear, "Can I have this recipe?"

The request for a recipe is a compliment to the cook. When a good recipe surfaces, it rapidly gets spread around like spilled sugar on the kitchen floor. It goes everywhere.

A few years ago I decided to use my mother's seafood casserole recipe for a luncheon I gave. Everyone seemed to enjoy it. Afterwards I told my mother about it and she said "I've never made it that way. Are you sure that is my recipe?"

"Well, it is in your handwriting," I told her.

"Mmm, I think I copied it out of a magazine when I was visiting you and forgot to take it home with me. It sounds delicious. Why don't you give it to me again. Maybe Sheila (my sister) can use it for that Bridal shower I'm helping her give."

Sheila did use the recipe for her party and subsequently gave out the recipe to three of her guests. One friend thought she'd try it out when her mother-in-law visited, who we found out later also loved the recipe and copied it down to use for her card club.

Back here in Nebraska, the recipe was also making the rounds. Two friends called me for the recipe after my luncheon. One wanted to make it for some relatives visiting from Wisconsin, both of whom took it down to make back home. My other friend served it at a buffet supper she was planning. Afterwards she told me four guests asked for the recipe.

Good food sure travels fast.

May 18, 1988

Good Food, or Just Good for You?

The most exciting thing we have to eat around here is a red pepper.

We have a lot of food because I just got home from grocery shopping, but it is all food that is healthful instead of, well, good.

At the store, I wasn't hungry and I was on one of my sensible kicks, trying to plan meals that are nutritious and delicious.

The cookies I did buy are almost gone, and I don't like them anyway. They're the inexpensive sandwich cookies. The kids open them, eat the centers and leave the cookie parts laying all around the house.

Now that I'm home and my refrigerator is full of green beans, broccoli and grapefruit, I wish I hadn't pushed my grocery cart right past the day-old bakery cart. One of those marked-down cherry-filled doughnuts would hit the spot (my hips) right now. I could eat an orange, but it wouldn't be the same.

The experts say never shop when you are hungry because you buy things you shouldn't. But if you shop when you aren't hungry, you don't buy things you shouldn't.

You should buy them, because when you get home from the store you'll want to eat something you shouldn't, and don't you think you should have something around for that?

If I'm lucky I can go to the grocery store hungry and leave full, because I've tried all the free samples. One day I had fresh squeezed orange juice and carrot sticks and dip in the produce section; a cocktail hot dog at the meat counter; a slice of pizza, a sampling of nachos and a portion of crab salad at the deli; and a miniature ice cream cone in the frozen foods aisle, topped off with a wedge of pound cake from the bakery and the beginning of a pound on me.

On the non-sample days I tell myself, "I ought to buy the kids a treat. I'll get some M&M cookies from the bakery." Then as I continue shopping I think, "I'm so hungry I'll just break off a little piece of a cookie."

Of course, one little piece is never enough so I have another and another. When I get home, the kids raid the bag. Instantly the cookies are all gone and I'm forced to say, "What happened to all those cookies? I bought two dozen."

I wonder if they know the truth.

My other problem with grocery shopping comes from visions of grandeur. For example, it's 5 p.m. on a Saturday and I've been meaning to go to the store all day. I never got around to it because I couldn't decide what I wanted to eat.

Suddenly the taste buds and I get a great idea for a meal.

It is probably something I've never made before. That doesn't matter – I'm going to eat it tonight. I hop into the car and speed off to the store.

I could be in and out of the store in a hurry if I just got what I needed for the evening meal, but I don't.

"As long as I'm here," I think, "I better get stuff for at least the next day."

Then I remember we are out of detergent and light bulbs, low on shampoo and toothpaste and that I promised to make a dessert for a meeting on Monday. Of course, we always need milk.

By the time I get home and get all the groceries in the house and put away, I have lost my zest for cooking.

Depending upon how strongly I hanker for this meal, I may continue and serve dinner fashionably late that night. Or I order a pizza.

February 4, 1987

Plan to Serve 'Simple Meal' Proves To Be a Contradiction in Terms

It was supposed to be a simple meal. John was out of town, and cousins Anne and Molly were spending the night at our house.

Anne said, "I like that taco salad you made, Aunt Kate, last time we were here." Since compliments on my cooking don't come too frequently, I answered, "You do? Well, maybe that's what we'll have tonight for supper."

Horan

Lately, I haven't been buying any kind of chips. I used to buy the most inexpensive ones, which continually caused Colleen to comment, "How come we never get any good chips?" Now, to avoid excessive calorie and junk food consumption, I don't buy any.

But that day I did buy taco-flavored corn chips to put on the salad. As it turned out, these chips became the jumping-off point for any hope of simplicity.

At 5 p.m., Maureen announced that Patrick and his friends had eaten almost all of the taco chips. I thought she was exaggerating, but a half-hour later, when I went out to the kitchen, I discovered that she wasn't. Not only were the majority of the chips gone, but the rest rapidly disappeared as we discussed our dinnertime options.

There were some taco shells in the cabinet, but one of the reasons I like to make taco salad instead of tacos is it isn't quite as messy as tacos. I decided I could make the salad and then everyone could make a taco with the taco shells and the pre-assembled ingredients. This seemed to be a satisfactory arrangement despite the running commentary about what stupid jerks Patrick and his friends were.

However, when the meal was completed and I looked at the taco salad-strewn table, I noticed that the taco shells weren't as adequate a replacement for the taco chips as I had thought.

I said to Anne, "I thought you liked taco salad, but all you ate was the grated cheese." "Oh, I just like the taco chips." she said.

Her sister, Molly, said, "The taco shells taste great with taco sauce on them; the rest of the salad is too healthy for me."

Mike was happy that not everyone ate their taco shells because he was able to stick the broken pieces into a gallon of milk. When I looked up from the newspaper I was reading and observed this activity I decided to begin cleaning up.

As I stood pouring the milk into glasses, scooping out the taco shell pieces and pouring the milk back into the carton – I figured it would give the morning cereal a Mexican flavor – Mike moved on to a jar of olives. He was just about done finishing off the olives when we were joined in the kitchen by the eight and under crowd who were wondering about dessert.

As long as the situation was already way out of my control I decided to let them make brownies from a brownie mix. Naturally a discussion ensued on who was going to do what.

Maureen is supposed to read aloud everyday, so I had her read the directions on the box to me. Machaela and Anne put the mix in the bowl, John sat on the counter to crack the egg, Mike pulled out a drawer to stand in to take his turn stirring and someone, I'm not sure who because I had to answer the phone and then tell Colleen it was for her, spilled a bottle of cooking oil on the floor. Baby Pete thought this was great because his walker really slid around on the slick floor.

At 11 p.m., when I was still wiping the oil off the floor, gathering up the brownie crumbs and dusting the bits of tomato and shredded lettuce off the chairs, I thought the saying "There's no such thing as a free lunch" pales when compared to the irony in my saying it will be a simple meal.

July 10, 1985

6 • YOU'RE CUTE AND THAT'S WHAT'S IMPORTANT

Readying for Church Is Hardly a Religious Experience

Have you ever sat in church waiting for your religious service to begin and a family walks in looking cleaned up and nicely dressed?

Did you think, "What a fine-looking family." That is what the mother wants you to think but what the onlooker should be thinking is that the mother needs prayers.

Let me take you behind the scenes: Unfortunately, getting ready for a religious experience is not even close to a religious experience. Quite the contrary, I feel that the devil has taken over my children. They, I'm sure, think Satan has disguised himself as their mother.

Monday through Friday everyone is up and at 'em, dressed for school. Spelling words are reviewed, milk or lunch money distributed, notes to the teacher are written, the washer and dryer are sloshing and tumbling respectively, and beds are sort of made.

The kitchen sink is stacked with cereal bowls, but at least the kitchen table is wiped off (in preparation for my four and under crowd, who have to wait for the second seating). All this takes place before 7:30 a.m.

This doesn't happen on Sunday mornings. No one moves.

The younger Cavanaughs do move but not far. They get out of bed and lie down in front of the television. The only activity is in the kitchen where cereal and milk are being spilled, the top of doughnuts are being eaten, and frozen orange juice is being over diluted.

When I do get out of bed, I convince myself not to let the mayhem disturb me for a few moments until after I relax and look at the newspaper. Suddenly, I realize those few moments have elapsed and now there isn't enough time to get ready for church. Although, I wonder if all the time in the world would be enough. This is when bedlam begins, especially if several churchgoers are still in bed.

I grew up in a family where church-going was important and being dressed for church was expected. I'm trying to raise a family in which church going is important and I expect them all to be dressed for it. I've given up on how I expect them to be dressed just as long as they are clothed.

Sunday morning is a good time for a mass bathing and nail clipping. I tell my little guys that Jesus' feelings will be hurt if they come to church with dirty fingernails. Mike doesn't believe me.

By the time we are finished, water, wet towels and piles of pj's and underwear are all over the bathroom floor and I don't need to bathe. I am cleaned by all the splashing.

The next crises are finding the right hair bow to go with a too-small dress Machaela wants to wear, finding an outfit for Maureen's impromptu overnight guest, Bridget, who slept in her soccer shirt, tracking down the socks for ten pairs of feet, and arguing with Pete about not wearing his Popsicle-stained "Born in the USA" muscle shirt.

I persuade Johnny that after church will be a better time to call and see if a friend can play. I convince Colleen that 15 minutes before church is not a good time to wash her hair.

I'm still yelling at Patrick to get out of bed, and I'm swearing under my breath but smiling artificially at John, the Dad, when he asks, "Do you remember where you put the Sunday envelopes?"

When everyone is sitting in the car, I start to get ready. How do I look after 60 seconds of primping? Just as you would expect.

The drive to church usually gives me an opportunity to collect myself unless there is some shock awaiting me in the back seat. Maybe Patrick will still be in the clothes he slept in, or Machaela didn't get her hair combed and no one has a brush or comb, or the baby is barefoot and it is 30 degrees out.

But when the prayers have been prayed and the hymns have been sung and we are on our way home again, I'm happy we made the effort. Especially if my guardian angel stayed behind to tidy up the house while we were out.

October 14, 1987

Kate Plays Landlady to a Stuffed Menagerie

The doll family is a family unlike any other in size, names, and adventures and they reside at our house.

They didn't take up residence all at once. It was one of those gradual situations we humans sometimes slip into, and before we are aware of it's existence, it is out of hand.

First came Chow Doggie also known as Puppy Chow. She (that distinction is important) is a stuffed dog given to Colleen at birth. Next came Giraffie 1 and 2 and Monk Monkaroo, gifts from Uncle Tom after an outing to the zoo. Then, as rapidly as the world population increased so did the Cavanaugh stuffed animal menagerie. Out of it all has emerged the Doll Family.

The members of this family are quite diverse and each has been given a name reflecting this diversity. Let me introduce you to a few of them. Meet Humpty, you have to shake him to get his bell to ring, and the Moppett puppet who's called Betty Veronica Puppity. Over there is the thumb sucking bear, Thumb Sucker.

On the couch are my favorites, the lover dogs, John and Kate. Sitting in the armchair are Richard the Racoon, who works at the neighborhood gift shop, and Dennised the Dog, who goes to kindergarten where he's known as Super Dennised.

Having this other family living in our house does pose a few problems. Their food bill is minimal, just a few crackers used at their St. Patrick's Day party. You should have seen Door Donkey, who's an Irish import, do the jig. However, clothing them has sometimes left baby Maureen sitting in her diapers while the doll family toddles about in her toddlerware.

The adventures of the Doll Family would make the Swiss Family Robinson seem to lack innovation. They go to Doll Family School where Teach Doll Family is the teacher, that is when he isn't curing the sick as the Doctor. My own children had a healthy winter but one bedroom was transformed into the sick ward for Helpbaby and

Hattie who had chicken pox. The pox looked amazingly like ink spots, and Juggly had Russian float (translated Russian flu).

Then, there is their traveling. The entourage has been to Bethlehem, Saudi Arabia, Lake Geneva, and Omaha in an airplane made of pillows and flown by Donald Duck, who is also a Captain of a boat which doubles as a Pepsi Carton.

Where do children get these fantastic imaginations? Where does it go when they grow up? I don't know if I ever had one as vivid but if I did, it escaped me in the last 25 years. Maybe that is what growing up does, we become so preoccupied with managing our daily chores we cease to create the sparkling fantasies of our childhood.

During each day my children evoke in me many feelings. Sometimes, I feel frustrated at the endless messes they make, fear at the fragility of life when they carelessly run into the street, guilt when I don't think I'm doing the right thing, depressed when I can't do something I want to do – but mostly I feel great joy.

As we approach what my daughter, Colleen, so aptly calls Happy Saint Mothers Day, I am grateful that I am a mother and the landlady to the Doll Family.

May 4, 1978

Reluctant Date, Mom Enjoy Prep's Prom

Last year in late January, when the envelope arrived in the mail I knew what it was. I had been waiting for it.

On the other hand, Patrick, who was in ninth grade, wasn't so eager to see it.

No it wasn't his report card. It was the invitation to Creighton Prep's Valentine Mom Prom. I had heard all about this mom dance from friends who have sons older than my first born, and they gave it rave reviews.

"You and Patrick have to go," my friend Janie said as I stood in her kitchen, looking at the picture pinned to the bulletin board of her and her son at last year's shindig. "We had a great time."

When the invitation arrived informing me of the time, date and cost of this dinner dance, I showed it to Patrick. I think he just mumbled and walked away.

When his Dad got home I showed the invitation to him.

"This sounds like a good time," he said. Then to Patrick, "Are you going to ask mom to the Mom Prom?" Patrick response was simply, "No," but I think he knew that the matter was not going to end as simply as his response and it didn't.

After dinner, John, the husband and father, effectively applied enough pressure to persuade Patrick to pop the question. I enthusiastically agreed to go, even though his invitation was qualified with, "No one else is going."

A few days later when I was filling out the RSVP card, Patrick told me again that "No one else is going."

"Oh, well, we are, because you invited me."

As the big day drew closer, once again I heard that "no one else is going."

"Have you asked around?" I wondered.

"I doubt they would hold this dance at Peony Park ballroom if no one went to it."

After this discussion he must have decided to see if it was going to be just us and the school disciplinarian dining and dancing, because a couple days later he began telling me of other guys who had succumbed to escorting their moms.

Once Patrick came to terms with this, I began thinking about what to wear. For once my wardrobe decision wasn't predominant in my thoughts. I had a pretty blouse and skirt I thought would be appropriately momish to wear but Patrick didn't have any clothes I considered appropriately sonish.

To the guy who considers tennis shoes with laces and a shirt with a collar formal wear I said, "You'll have to wear a sport coat and tie."

"Are you kidding?" he replied, with a look that suggested I had told him he had to go out dressed like the king of Ak-sar-ben.

I considered buying him a sport coat, but he discouraged me with the logic, "I'll never wear it again." This was true, because he was growing one to two inches every week.

I opted to get him new pants and a shirt, to have him wear one of his dad's ties and to borrow a sport coat from the brother of a friend. He wasn't happy about this idea, "I bet no one will be wearing a sport coat," he said.

"Put your money where your mouth is," I answered. "I'll bet you $100 (I felt safe in risking this bet) that most everyone will be wearing ties and sport coats or nice sweaters."

On the evening of the dance even my reluctant escort had to admit it was a good time. We ate, danced and had our picture taken. To my surprise, I was introduced by my date to all the guys he had been telling me all sorts of things about since the school year began.

The time for this year's Valentine's mom-prom is here again. Even though I have never collected last year's bet winnings, I have collected an invitation for this year's dance.

My escort isn't enthusiastic, but he is a little less reluctant. He has stopped growing long enough to get his own sport coat and now realizes that dressing up for a few hours won't permanently disfigure him.

Also, all his friends also have to go. And I said since he has his driver's permit now I'll let him drive us there.

February 10, 1988

5-Year-Old's Eyes Can Make a Mom Forget Strait-Laced Shoe Budget

Within the year, in a darkened closet underneath some worn out sweat pants and surrounded by balls of dust peeking out all aglow will be the had-to-have, glow-in-the-dark high top tennis shoes.

Mike would argue until tears came out of his all-so-endearing and irresistible 5-year-old eyes that this is not possible, but I'd swear on a pile of discarded Nikes, Reeboks, and Kangaroos that it is.

However, even this oath did not bar me from footing the bill for his new footings.

We were on a school preparedness outing, which included purchasing school supplies, getting haircuts, and buying shoes.

As you can imagine, at this point in our travels the checkbook balance was in decline and the credit card balance was on the rise.

As we drove along to the shoe shop, I began my "This is what is going to happen next" lecture.

"Not everyone will be getting shoes today. Mike and Pete, we just got those rocket ship high tops for you and they are still in good shape. You don't need anything new right now but John does. So you'll be good in the store, OK?"

This idea seemed agreeable to the boys for the rest of the ride in the car, but I guess that to them two minutes is long enough to be agreeable.

Soon we arrived at the store where you take your shoes off and stand on the metal measuring contraption. It communicated with Mom's purse saying, "This foot has expanded like the Incredible Hulk, and it can't be stuffed into the outrageously overpriced dress shoes you bought for the one dress up occasion last spring. You'll have to buy a new pair of overpriced dress shoes to wear once and then grow out of."

This is when Mike asked, "Can I get some new shoes too?"

When I reminded him about our conversation in the car he said, "That was before I saw my most favorite shoes ever."

Any recollection of our non-purchase agreement dimmed as the glow in Mike's eyes brightened over the leopard design, glow-in-the-dark high-top sneakers.

Vacillation began. I crept away from an absolute "no" to "I doubt they have your size."

"Let's check," Mike pleaded, leading me over to the stack of boxes.

In a few moments he was laced to above his ankle bones in leopard canvas. My bargaining chips were about to be cashed in at the checkout counter.

I began a discussion with myself:

I don't really want to spend any more money today.

If we get the shoes maybe Mike will let up on asking if he can get a parrot.

But if I get the shoes he'll think he can have anything if he is relentless.

Maybe I should tell him he has to wait until they are on sale – but there's only one pair left in his size. If we wait, they'll be gone and he'll be heartbroken and he is such a good guy. And he just got over the disappointment when I told him he couldn't get a monkey even though he said it wouldn't be any trouble because he'd always carry it on his shoulder. "Mom, are you in a trance or what?" Maureen asks.

She is waiting her turn to work me over about buying a pair of shoes that remind me of a guy who'd clean his fingernails with a switch blade and cracks safes for a living.

"I guess we'll get the shoes," I tell Mike.

"Thank you Mommy," Mike answered. "I'll pick up toys in the basement to earn the dollars to pay for them."

"Good idea," I agreed, wondering how to deduct his earnings from my Visa bill.

Buying the shoes turned out to be the right decision. The shoes have become our family's entertainment.

Mike takes anyone who will go into the dark bathroom and demonstrates how the shoes glow in the dark. Maureen and Machaela, using one shoe each, did a bedtime dance performance in the dark for the little guys.

Pete can't wait to go to the Halloween Haunted houses this year. He says the ghosts will be scared when they see Mike's glowing shoes. And a scared ghost has to be worth at least the price of the shoe box.

September 21, 1988

• •

Giving Up TV Left More Time for Fighting

We gave up watching television during Lent.

I wish I could say we didn't miss it. I wish I could say our family read the classics instead of watching Bill Cosby, and that we had long conversations about our hopes, dreams and feelings instead of grunting at each other during commercials of "Family Ties," but I can't.

The only reading that increased was of the TV program listings. The kids read it and then told me what great shows they had missed. As for improved communications, the lack of TV watching only freed up more time for fighting.

We didn't dive right into this penance. When Lent began, nobody had any ideas, good or bad. So John and I told the kids we were giving up television for a week. After the week passed, everyone felt they had been TV-less long enough and it was time to give up something else, like washing dishes.

"Let's keep the television off," I said.

"You've got to be kidding!" a chorus of protesters shouted. "You said we'd give it up for a week and see how it went."

"It went great so we're going to keep it off until Easter," I responded powerfully. "You can watch Sundays and on St. Patrick's Day."

"But the only thing on Sunday is Mass for shut-ins and other religious shows," Maureen said.

"The ban on TV doesn't include watching movies on the video recorder," Patrick said confidently.

"Yes, I'm afraid it does."

"Well," Colleen said, "if we have to make this extraordinary sacrifice, Dad can't watch the news or sports."

"That's right," I said, and John never turned on the TV – until Corazon Aquino took over the Philippines, the stock market started breaking records and the NCAA playoffs began.

"A man's got to be informed, right?" was his justification. That may be true, but I'm not sure why he needs to be informed about basketball.

At first, it was a pleasant relief not to have to compete with the blasting box. And since I never seemed to see the shows I liked, I doubted I would miss TV. But I did miss it.

I missed seeing what Jan Pauley was wearing each morning on the "Today" show. I missed guessing the puzzles on the "Wheel of Fortune," and I really missed keeping track of my soap opera characters.

Most of all, I missed using the television as a baby-sitter. At 3 p.m. every afternoon when the kids are losing their good nature, it is nice to have He-Man and She-Ra and the "Masters of the Universe" program do the entertaining, instead of leaving it to the plastic 6-inch He-Man and She-Ra figures and me.

When I asked the kids how they benefited from this television-less experience, Machaela, who is 7, said, "Well, TV is bad for you. I wonder why they invented something bad for you like TV?"

Said Colleen: "I learned that next year I'm going to think of something to do for Lent before you get any more great ideas for us."

April 2, 1986

. . . .

Can a Parent Ever Be Ready for Son's Driver's License Test?

Two years ago I didn't think I ever would be ready to have a teen-age driver.

One year ago when Patrick turned 15 I still didn't think I was ready but I realized I better get ready because Patrick was eligible to get his learner's driving permit and in a year's time he'd be able to get his license.

Now that year has passed, and whether I was ready or not, the acquisition of a driver's license was unavoidable.

Patrick turned 16 last week.

While I was waiting for his birth it seemed the eleven days he was overdue from the Doctor's predicted due date were the longest ones of my life. Once he arrived, time passed at a record pace only to step on the brakes when he was fifteen years, eleven months and two weeks old.

Those last days crawled by as Patrick marked them off on the calendar, waiting to clip another link in the chain of dependence. For Patrick a driver's license meant independence and he was most eager to have it.

This past year as Patrick practiced driving, I rode shotgun, avoiding the temptation to grab the steering wheel, stomping on imaginary brakes, and alternating between cursing and praying under my breath. I wanted out of the car.

So when the big day arrived I was mentally ready but physically weak. It helped that I had been broken in gradually by a stream of Patrick's buddies who had made this rite of passage last winter or spring. Several times a week one of the guys would pull into the driveway looking for Patrick, and then they would be off, going about the business of being teenagers.

At first these outings required me to take a gulp of courage and ask a big heap of questions. Gradually I relaxed and now I can let him go out in a car with friends after asking only a small heap of questions and experiencing just a slight elevation of my heart rate.

When I picked Patrick up at school to take the test, I was as excited as he was. I was also nervous. Maybe I was thinking about our new insurance rates. He assured me after a year of practice driving and taking the driver's training course he was prepared.

"Don't you think you should read over the rules of the road testing manual first?" I suggested.

"The written part is kind of tricky. What if you get this question: If you enter an intersection as the light turns yellow should you:

A) Drive up on the median to get out of the way?

B) Step on the gas, honk your horn and wave a red handkerchief out the window?"

"I'd answer yes to both of the above," Patrick said.

He managed to get through the written part and then the examiner took Patrick out in the car to drive. I was optimistic until they returned and only the examiner came back in the building.

"Didn't he pass?" I asked.

"No, he only did one thing wrong but I couldn't pass him."

"What was the mistake?" I asked.

"He was speeding," the examiner explained.

I left and got into the car where Patrick was waiting.

"Speeding on your driver's test? You are lucky you didn't get stopped by the police."

I was tempted to also say, "Couldn't you have failed for something run of the mill like not using your turning signals or driving over the curb?" I didn't. After all, Patrick isn't a run of the mill fellow, nor would I want him to be.

I also don't want him to speed, and he didn't the next day when he went back and passed the test. According to Pete and Mike, who had their first ride with big brother on the way to soccer practice, "Patrick drove real slow."

More experienced parents of teen drivers tell me this is the honeymoon period. I wonder how many errands he can run for me before the honeymoon is gone and so is Patrick, driving off in my car.

October 19, 1988

Slow Service Steams the Customers at 'Cavanaugh Cafe'

Everyone has his own agenda. I know I do. My Maureen, who is 9, certainly does.

Most of the time her agenda is pretty free-wheeling and easy to live with. Once in a while, she gets an idea on how she would like things to be done and, boy, we had better do it her way.

She had one of her ideas the other night. Our good friend, Molly, was over for a casual summer dinner. Also visiting for the day were two cousins, Molly and Anne.

In preparation for the meal, I instructed Maureen, Machaela and Anne to set the table on the screened porch. They did this, and a few minutes later Maureen appeared in the kitchen with some paper and a pen.

"What are we having for dinner?" she asked.

After I listed the proposed courses, she asked Molly to write everything down for her because she couldn't spell marinated vegetables: "First write entree, and then everything else."

A few minutes later, John entered the kitchen carrying the meat he had cooked on the grill and we were ready to sit down to eat, or so I thought.

As I called everyone to come to the porch for dinner, Maureen was running back and forth by the porch doors yelling to everyone that she wasn't ready.

"You're ruining everything," she told the kids.

"See what's wrong with her," I told Colleen.

After checking, Colleen came back and said, "She's mad because we didn't see her sign taped to the door that says, 'Wait to be seated.'"

"Oh, well, everyone go back into the family room," I instructed.

John, Molly and I proceeded to get the food organized with the intention of fixing everyone's plates when we noticed Maureen throwing herself up and down on the couch.

"Maybe we better see what she wants," John suggested.

"We're trying to have a restaurant and nobody is cooperating," Maureen wailed.

"We can still do it if you stop carrying on and hurry up before the food gets cold," I told her.

She calmed down long enough to finish writing her menus, and then we all had to pretend that we were patrons at the Cavanaugh Cafe.

When we arrived at her specified entrance, I said, "We'd like a table for 12."

"Do you have a reservation? What's your name?" Maureen asked.

After I told her my name she looked at her list, shook her head and said, "I don't believe you have a reservation. We can't seat you." Then she looked at our guest and asked her name.

When Molly told her, Maureen said, "Yes, your name is on here."

"We're with her," I said.

"Her reservation is only for three. You can't all be with her," Maureen responded.

I was getting rather steamed up as I visualized the steam rising from our corn on the cob.

"What other names are on your list. We'll change ours."

She read, "Ally Sheedy."

"I'll be her," cousin Molly said.

"Katherine Hepburn."

"That's me," I said. Then she read names of members of a rock group who Johnny and Mike chose to be. I said, "The rest of these people are our fans. Can we please sit down now?"

"Of course," Maureen answered. "Anne and Machaela, show our guests to the table."

"At last," I thought, "we get to eat."

But we didn't. First we had to read the menu and then wait to be served. Once again, things didn't go as smoothly as Maureen thought it should. All the orders were different. We all wanted corn, but some wanted meat and no rice and some wanted rice and no meat. I just wanted to get out of there.

Finally, to my amazement, we all had plates of food in front of us. And just as I was congratulating myself for passing another test of motherhood, Maureen announced, "For dessert we're having blueberry cobbler. I'll serve it as soon as I beat the whipping cream with the electric mixer."

No longer did it seem like we were engaged in a young girl's creative endeavors. It seemed more like a plot to push me off that narrow edge I spend each day teetering on.

After regaining my composure, I said to Maureen, "Either you hire me as the pastry chef for the Cavanaugh Cafe and I fix the cobbler or we leave your establishment without leaving a tip."

Now that this gala event is over, do I look back and smile?

Let me put it this way. This is one time when the story is funnier if you weren't there.

July 30, 1986

· ·

Welcome to Patrick's Island

Patrick hasn't been sleeping in his own bed for a few weeks now. As a matter of fact, he's not doing anything you would do ordinarily in a bedroom like sleep, change your clothes or sit at your desk and draw a picture. It's OK, though, because his room is no longer the bedroom of a nine-year-old boy. It is now "Gilligan's Island."

Patrick has an enthusiasm that only can be described as Gilliganitis. The TV show comes on each weekday at 3:30 p.m. and Patrick likes to plan his afternoon accordingly.

Since I'm on an anti-TV campaign, I ordinarily wouldn't approve of such an addiction. A day rarely goes by without my saying, "Turn off that TV before your brains turn into mush."

One of the reasons I object to television is that it limits the imagination and discourages creativity. If you saw Patrick's room you would understand why I don't call a halt to his love affair with 20-year-old reruns of the adventures of seven people stranded on a desert island.

With dental floss, scotch tape, masking tape, ribbon, paper from a sketching tablet and his new watercolor paint set, Patrick has transformed his bedroom into Gilligan's Island.

When you enter his bedroom, you can almost hear the theme song, "Sit right back and you'll hear a tale of a fateful ship . . . "

There's a dental floss suspension bridge connecting the twin beds; extended by scotch tape from the ceiling light fixture is the professor's house and garage, but the professor isn't home. He's over at his laboratory located on the left bed next door to Ginger (the movie star) and Mary Anne's house and across the street from the restaurant, which is surrounded by fruit trees that provide the food for the restaurant.

On the other bed is the house of the millionaire and his wife, Mr. and Mrs. Howell. Down the road, which is taped to the bedspread, is Gilligan and Skipper's house. To the left is the airport and hanger complete with paddle-power airplanes that only fly a half-mile before they get too tired of pumping.

The people on Gilligan's Island have become more than fictional characters to our family. Their names are interjected into our daily conversation. Whenever I'm complaining about high prices, Patrick says, "Gee, if you were as rich as Mr. Howell you wouldn't need to worry."

When the girls play dress up, they argue about who gets to be Ginger, the movie star. If Johnny starts digging up a plant Patrick tells him that the professor says you never eat a plant unless you are sure it's not poisonous.

The Gilligan era probably will come to an end when the networks rearrange their afternoon programming, but I'm not worried about a drought in Patrick's creativity. He's already using the expressions of Commandant Klink on "Hogan's Heroes."

September 1, 1982

. . . .

Wedding Bells Aren't Chiming in Boys' Plans for Life

The car radio was on.

"That's pretty music," I commented to the little guys with me. Then 5-year-old Mike said, "That's wedding music." I was surprised to hear him say that but he was right. It was wedding music.

"Do you like it?" I asked him.

"Yeah, it sounds nice," he answered.

"Would you like to have that music played at your wedding?" I wondered aloud as I silently began planning Mike's wedding, reception, pre-nuptial dinner, my dress, and who would be just the right bride for my wonderful boy.

But Mike ended my daydream by saying, "I'm not getting married."

"You aren't?"

"No, I'm not."

"You don't have to get married until you're bigger. Maybe you'll change your mind."

"I can't get married," Mike replied. "I'm going to get a lot of jobs."

"What sort of jobs are you going to get?" I asked.

"I'm going to work at the gas station, the hair cut place, and the grocery store," was his answer. Those are the three places he goes and they all look like interesting places to work.

That evening I told John about Mike's plans for life.

"You aren't getting married?" he asked his young son.

"No, I'm not."

"Don't you want to have children?"

"No," answered Mike, who at this point was doing flips on the family room couch. "I don't want to have kids, they bother me."

"Where are you going to live?" John asked.

"I'm going to buy this house and live here."

"That's a good plan," John and I answered as we wondered where we would live.

Since that day, Mike has changed his mind about the house. He was disappointed with the size of our Christmas tree. He wanted to buy the 11-foot one and we got the 9-foot one because we couldn't remember how high our ceiling is. When we got home we realized the bigger one would have worked, and Mike let us know he wasn't happy about the tree.

"When I grow up I'm getting a big house with lots of room with real high ceilings."

"Who is going to live with you if you don't get married?"

Mike pointed to 4-year-old Pete, who was agreeing with him about the tree's size.

"And you can, too," he said to me, "if you are still alive."

Even though Pete already has a prospective spouse, he claims it isn't going to work out. The other night, Maureen returned home from babysitting our next door neighbor's children with the message, "Pete, Annie says you two are in a fight."

"That's right," Pete said. "Annie thinks we are in a fight because she wants to get married but I can't get married."

"Why not?" Maureen asked as the rest of the family strained their ears to hear Pete's thoughts on the subject.

"Because I'm going to be a scientist and scientists can't get married."

That makes sense doesn't it?

For one of Patrick's 11th grade classes, he had to project his life's activities into the future and write a resume and a letter applying for a job. He wrote seeking a job as an international airline pilot. In the resume where he was to include relevant facts, he stated, "I am single and could devote all my time to flying for the airlines without anyone wanting me home all the time."

I should have pointed out to Patrick that in the mid 90's the chances of a wife sitting home waiting for her husband are remote. Patrick could find his wife up in the cockpit with him.

What did occur to me was Patrick's aversion to marriage was my third strike in the inning of life when I become the mother of the groom. Luckily, I have two more sons.

John, who is 8, says he doesn't know yet, if he'll get married, and Matthew may get married someday but right now the only girl for him is his mom. That must be the reason he calls me Mrs. Cavanaugh.

January 11, 1989

New Phone Technology Has Familiar Ring

Until I was about 10 years old, we didn't have dial phones.

It wasn't quite like it was on "Lassie." We didn't crank the phone up and say, "Jennie give me the General Store." We were much more cosmopolitan. There was a telephone company in the next town filled with operators who would say, "Number please" when you picked up the phone. I would say either 3854 which was

Croy

my friend Catherine's number, 2398 which was Mona and Pam's number (they lived kitty-corner to us), or 4048m2, which was Cindy's number. Her family lived out in the country, so they had to have a party line.

Then one day everything was switched to dial phones. We got a dial tone and prefix added to our number. Ours was Juno 4.

We thought it was a real dumb name. Why couldn't it have been something more fashionable sounding like Magnolia 3 or Chantilly 5.

Best of all was the rotary dialing. We took turns holding the receiver button down and practicing dialing numbers.

Coming back to 1988, people have pleaded with us to do something about the phone. I was always hearing, "A family the size of yours, with only one phone line coming into the house, without a call-waiting button anywhere to be pressed, is impossible to call. The line is always busy."

I hesitated to make the change. All that beeping and interrupting whenever I spoke to other people who had call waiting made me nervous. I always wanted to end my conversation in the middle of a three-syllable word and let the party go on to answer the other call from someone who might be important.

I didn't think I got enough important calls to warrant having an extra line busting into my conversations all the time.

What if I had call waiting and I finally was having an important conversation?

Maybe it would be from a sweepstakes spokesman telling me where to pick up my prize money, when in the middle of his directions the phone would beep and a little voice would come on asking for three-year-old Pete.

Those notions are now gone. Not only have I sunk to that mode of telephoning, I have succumb even further. We also got a teen line.

The day I realized it was time to plug into telephone expansion, I couldn't use the phone to place the order. I was waiting for a call, so I couldn't make the call because I didn't want to tie up the line.

Several other people in the house also wanted to make calls but I wouldn't let them. This meant the line was open to our house and friends were keeping it warm. However, I was telling them to keep it short, real short. All they were allowed to say was, "I can't talk now, my mom is waiting for a call."

A few seconds later another friend would call. As the kids popularity seemed to be escalating, my policies' popularity was rapidly de-escalating.

The next morning I ordered a teen line, which comes with call waiting and three way calling and call waiting for my own phone. The family was jubilant and quickly called their friends with the good news. Then they all had advice as to where the new teen line phone jacks should be installed. These suggestions all sounded the same, "Put it in my room."

That decision was eliminated when the telephone man came. "Your house is already wired for two lines. If you would like I can easily hook up your second line to all your existing phone jacks and then you'd have two lines throughout the house.

"That's a great idea. What about phones?"

"You'll have to get different phones with two lines in order to use the second line."

That's what we did but so far I have only purchased one extra phone and it is in the kitchen. "That's not a convenient place to carry on a conversation," Colleen has informed me.

The little guys who never used the phone before are having a wonderful time. They call each other between the new and old lines. They call our old number when Colleen is visiting with her friends and then fall on the floor laughing when she answers the call waiting call and realizes it is her young siblings.

History repeats itself once again.

October 12, 1988

Milestones for Teens Part of Life's Canvas

Writing this column is fun because I get to tell you all about my children and their misadventures. In a way my columns make the diary I've always felt I should keep but never have.

Recently, the kids went through some of my old columns that were written when the big kids were little kids and the other five were still waiting in the wings. We had fun reminiscing.

In the past few months I have had two experiences, one with Patrick, who is 16, and the other with Colleen, 14. If those experiences are left untold, the picture of my life painted by my columns would not be a complete canvas. My two oldest more clearly defined themselves in two very different situations, and I was challenged to grow and redefine myself as a mother.

In September and October, Colleen played the role of Jennie Mae Laymen in the Omaha Community Playhouse's production of "The Diviners." In late November, Patrick flew his solo flight and obtained his student pilot's license. Both of these are fabulous accomplishments. I hope you think it is okay to say this even if I am their mother.

I told everyone during the run of "The Diviners" that it was an outstanding play, rich in language and warm with friendship and humor. It would have been that even if Colleen was not a part of it. But because she was in it, the play was even more special.

Seeing my daughter perform on the stage in a dramatic and beautiful role was an emotional experience. Colleen knows she doesn't need to be on the stage to elicit love, praise, and affection from her parents – I love her even when she leaves the house wearing long underwear hanging out of the boxer shorts – although we certainly glopped it on her. We couldn't help it; I was like a glass sitting under an open spigot of Coca-Cola syrup and carbonated water. I was gushing and bubbling over.

I realized she was doing something I have never done and probably could never do. Colleen became her own person through her own doing. It felt good to see that.

Apparently, acting is her love just as flying appears to be Patrick's. He began taking flying lessons when he was twelve, using our money and money he earned mowing lawns to pay for them. This fall, when he turned 16, he became eligible for a student license. He took a ground school class in addition to his flying lessons, had his physical exam and then he was ready for his solo voyage.

I wasn't sure I was quite as ready, but there was nothing I could do about it. Eventually, I knew my hand-wringing had to stop and I had to let him take flight – literally – from my runway.

On the appointed day we all went, carrying a camera and camcorder to the airport. Later, Patrick said that from the air it looked like a huge crowd standing on the ground looking up. I thought the same thing, although it was just his parents, and seven younger brothers and sisters. The question that went through my mind – along with several Hail Marys – was what course are the rest of these people going to chart?

As John and I stood watching Patrick make his takeoff, bank to the left and then direct the plane on its course high in the sky, we were thrilled and proud of him. I also experienced a rush of emotion that ranged from remembering when he was born (that one always surfaces at times like this) to absolute terror, which caused Maureen to comment, "Are you going to start crying now like you did at Colleen's play?"

I would have cried, except the tears would have clouded my vision and I didn't want to take my eyes off the plane.

Since that day, Patrick has flown solo again. He said he flew over the house. I was excited to hear this even though the idea gives me the willies.

December 28, 1988

7 • MY POST GRADE SCHOOL DEGREE

Cranky Children: Some Mornings, Only a Family Could Love Them

Machaela seemed pretty calm when she got home from school, which was surprising. When she left this morning she had the crank-a-lu-la's.

It started when I woke her up and she said, "Too early, I'm too tired to get up." I felt the same way, but I said, "Once you're up for a little while you'll feel better."

"You always say that," she answered, "and it is not true."

I gave her a uniform blouse and her uniform and then ran off to light some fireworks under Patrick to get him moving, only to be called back to Machaela's room by the sounds of a fit in progress. I had given her "the wrong stupid blouse; did you think I was Maureen?"

Everyone came downstairs but Machaela, who was lying on the landing at the top of the stairs carrying on. The heel of her sock was on the front instead of the back of her foot and she couldn't fix it. Socks have always been a problem for her. When she was in preschool, car-pools loaded with 4-year-olds would be cooling their wheels in our driveway while I'd run up and down the stairs seeking the acceptable sock.

Finally Machaela was ready to go. My nerves also were ready for her to go. When she reached the front door, she saw Colleen and Maureen waiting by the sidewalk instead of by the door.

Her reaction, a hysterical "They're not waiting for me!" caused me to run to the door to make assurances that they were. Out she ran, yelling the whole way. I made the mistake of yelling after her: "I put your census card in your bag."

"I can't hear you," she screamed. Colleen did hear me and tried to show Machaela the card, which made Machaela turn on Colleen, "I knew it was in there, why are you showing me something I already know?"

Now I was getting worried that they would miss the bus, so I went out on the lawn in my nightgown to tell them to get going. Colleen, who probably wondered why she couldn't have been an only child, grabbed Machaela's hand and dragged her down the street.

After school, I asked Colleen when Machaela calmed down. She replied, "Well, half-way to the bus stop, she said she was sick. So I told her to go back home, but she didn't want to."

"Instead she put her backpack around her neck and started screaming again, saying she was choking to death. But then the bus came, she got on and she was all smiles. It doesn't make any sense, does it?"

But it does make sense. When we go out in the world, we have to behave. Home is where we can have our fits and still be loved. That's where I have mine.

At the age of 6, Machaela knows this. She knows we don't love her fits, but she knows we love her just as she loves us when it is our turn to be out of sorts.

In a family, everyone seems to have his day. But after today, I hope I don't get the chance tomorrow to love someone in spite of himself.

September 19, 1985

Kids' School Routine Is Never That for Mom

Whew!! School has been open for a couple of weeks and I think we are into a routine, but just barely.

Since I had expected the baby to be born right before school started, I was remarkably well organized – for me.

I took Colleen and Johnny to the doctor for physicals. We all went to the dentist, everyone had a haircut. We made a trip to the school uniform store. I had Patrick's pants hemmed.

One morning we went to the shoe store and then to buy all the school supplies. I came home from that outing out of patience and even more out of money, but before I collapsed on the couch, we organized the school bags.

I registered John and the girls. I took Patrick to his book sale, and arranged car pools to John's kindergarten and Mike's preschool.

When I had all these things accomplished I breathed a sigh of relief and went to the hospital to give birth and rest up.

After reading that list, don't you agree my family's first day of school should have run smoothly? If not, you most likely have children in school, or had at one time.

You know that no matter how prepared you are for the first day of school, you will still be overwhelmed with things to do for the second day of school.

I am considering having a rubber stamp made of our biographical data. I'll use it to stamp the census cards that parents are asked to fill out for each child every school year.

Although it isn't difficult to write down our name, address, place of employment, etc, I have a terrible time completing the cards.

I think the repetition gets to me. How come if I write down my child's name on the front of the card, the people in authority forget whose card it is by the time they look at the back, so I have to write the name again?

Book covering is another jagged stone on my path to a smooth start of school. On the first three days of school, Colleen, Maureen and Machaela each brought home several books to be covered.

At first we used nice bookcovers we had purchased. When they were gone, we used grocery bags. When we ran out of bags, we had to borrow more from our neighbor.

One of the borrowed bags had a Statue of Liberty design, which Maureen insisted I use to cover one of her books.

Like filling in census cards, covering books isn't too difficult – with the exception of trying to center the Statue of Liberty on the front of a social studies text – but it is time consuming.

I feel guilty about spending so much time looking at the outside of the books, when I could be looking inside to see what my children will be learning.

This school year the kids decided they wanted to take lunch instead of buying it every day.

I preferred having them buy lunch, so that I never had to worry about buying lunch food. My student body said they never packed lunches before because, "There's never anything good around here to take for lunch."

So this year I've gone to the grocery store almost every day to get lunch fixings. We still don't have anything good to take for lunch, because it all gets eaten as after school snacks.

Adjusting to a new school year usually takes some time. I figure we ought to have things running smoothly just in time for Christmas vacation.

September 24, 1986

She Needn't Have Studied . . . Homework Helper Repeating Grades

A terrifying thought just occurred to me: I have eight children.

I already knew I had eight children. What I realized is that I have eight children who will have to do science fair projects, term papers and relief maps.

If I had known when I was going through school that I would be repeating grades kindergarten through 12 over and over, I surely wouldn't have studied so hard. I wouldn't have holed up in my room doing geometry problems in 1963 when I could have been cruising Main Street and the Dog 'n' Suds Drive-In looking for boys, had I known I'd be taking the class again in 1988.

There is homework, and then there is Homework. I can handle the spelling words, math problems and grammar. It is the Homework with a capital H, which I can't help do while I read the newspaper, cook dinner, or talk on the phone, that is the problem.

It is these big assignments that set my teeth to grinding and my heart to pounding.

Whenever one of my offspring announces it is time to do a science fair project, write a term paper with bibliography or build a model of the Alamo with Q-tips, I panic.

I get a tremendous desire to wish it all away, which I do until the avoidable becomes unavoidable and the assignment is due.

My problem is I'm not interested enough in white mice to invite them into my home and then act as their fitness coach.

I don't have the time to assemble scraps of paper with valuable research recorded illegibly on why Charles Lindbergh's plane was controversial.

I'm not good at constructing a historical landmark out of materials otherwise used for dental hygiene or making frozen treats with Kool-Aid.

Naturally, these assignments shouldn't be my problem. After all, my child is the one who was assigned the projects in school, right?

How come I don't believe that logic?

The student is the one who has to be in charge of the projects – the mom or dad can't take over. The child may be forever blowing in the wind if he does not get to conduct his experiment – what happens to an electric fan when you stick stuff in its blades – the way he wanted to do it.

I'd just as soon choose the project and do the whole thing myself, but it doesn't work that way. I always end up doing it their way.

We also do it according to their timetable, which is always at the last minute. Of course, I'm told it is my fault when I get hysterical because we have six hours to conduct a six-week experiment.

"You should have told me to start sooner," the student says as we drive around trying to find a store still open at 11 p.m. that sells the mixture needed to simulate a volcanic eruption from a model made of crumpled and painted grocery sacks.

"This really isn't my problem and I should forget helping out and let you suffer the consequences," I say. We both know this will never happen.

The moral to this is aimed at teachers with grading pens poised. Remember that behind every project, term paper and experiment is a parent who wants a good grade.

March 9, 1988

Dash for Picnic Supplies Costs $48.63

"Can we go to the store?" Colleen asked the other night.

"Do we have to?" I asked. It was after 8 p.m., I had just finished cleaning up after my kitchen cleanup crew, and I was ready to hang up my towel for the day.

"We have our school picnic tomorrow and I don't have anything good to take for lunch," she said.

I agreed that was a dilemma, and off we went to the store.

No big deal, you are thinking. This should be a quick shot in and out of the store for a bag of chips and some Ho-Ho's or Twinkies.

Well, you are thinking wrong, as all Colleen's classmates and their parents who were also picking up picnic supplies will confirm. There is no such thing as a quick grocery shopping trip.

I believe this picnic lunch cost me $48.63, because once I was in the store I remembered all sorts of things we needed.

If we needed them, what's the problem? We may have needed them, but I intended to do without until my next shopping trip. Now we not only bought the items ahead of schedule but we also ate them ahead of schedule.

We are at the height of the field trip season, which means an appropriate kid's version of a gourmet lunch has to be prepared for each school outing.

Maureen, who is not a big eater, makes me wonder if she plans to set up concession stands on her outings. The other day she gave me her list of items to get for her lunch, and that night she put it together.

She made a turkey sandwich with sliced $3.98-a-pound turkey from the deli. She also packed a container of yogurt, fruit roll-ups, taco chips, two cans of pop and strawberries. And then she had a fit when someone opened her bag of chocolate kisses and smuggled out several pieces.

When she finished with her larder, she put the bag in the refrigerator – then forgot to take it in the morning. I was a bit put out about this, but I forget things, too.

The week before, I was supposed to buy a can of pop for Maureen to take to school to drink while her class was treated to a movie. But I forgot, so I promised I'd buy pop and bring it over when I picked up John's kindergarten car pool.

And even though Maureen asked me several times, left a note on my pillow, and even called from school to remind me, I completely forgot until two hours later when I was getting the boys haircuts and Pete started begging for a can of pop from the machine.

I quickly bought a can, even though it wasn't the brand Maureen requested, then raced to school with it just as the movie started.

It would be nice if the extra food I buy for one of the kids' excursions would last for someone else's, but it doesn't work that way. They never want the same things.

John wanted to get a cherry pie for the zoo trip. Mike thought John should get Hostess cupcakes, the chocolate ones, but John didn't want to. Mike thought we should get them anyway. He expressed that opinion so effectively – he began opening the box in the store – that I agreed we needed them.

Of course, it doesn't matter at all because the cupcakes disappeared shortly after they arrived.

For her field trip Colleen requested Perrier water, which I think is a ridiculous purchase. I'm just not cool. But I decided to be extravagant and get it for her.

When she took two bottles of the bottled highfalutin water to school, a teacher at first thought she had bottles of beer. So for her class picnic Colleen opted to bring something more easily recognized: Classic Coke.

May 20, 1987

Mom Finished Her Homework in the Eighth Grade

School is a great idea for children, not only for the obvious reason that it gets them out of the house every day, but because they learn all sorts of things they need to know, such as that their pants have to be really narrow at the ankle or the cuffs rolled up.

In the morning our house is hectic. The children get up, get dressed, eat, find their book bags, lunch money, lunches or show-and-tell items, then leave.

For the next several hours, the confusion is cut in half. This sigh of relief is necessary to get ready for the post-school activities that include homework.

As soon as my students get home, I start asking about homework. I would tell them to immediately get started on the assignments, but even I know that is a crazy notion.

There's no way any of my family can start homework right away. First they need to scatter their school books over the table, drop coats and gym clothes on a chair or the floor, mess up the kitchen getting something to eat and finally flop in front of the television.

While all of this is going on, I'm inquiring about the homework. The usual response is, "How come you never buy anything good to eat?" or "Isn't there any more strawberry jelly?"

During dinner I again ask the children what homework they have. Patrick says he has "Stuff" to do. Maureen says, "You already asked me that."

"Yes," I say, "and you never answered me."

Machaela says, "Spelling words. I already told you that." And Colleen says, "Everything."

When they are finally ready to begin homework, I want to read the newspaper, so I listen to Machaela's spelling words between reading letters to Ann Landers and have Maureen practice reading on the "Hints to Heloise" column.

When Colleen comes downstairs and asks for help with social studies, I say, "Why don't you ask Dad for help?"

"Couldn't you just do it?" she begs. "Last time I asked Dad what year the Civil War was, he made me read three different articles in the encyclopedia, he got out maps showing scenes of battles and talked forever about something called the Emancipation Proclamation."

Just as I'm thinking about going to bed, Patrick brings me his "stuff" to look over. Usually it is in English grammar that he needs help.

Since I'm tired, I tell him I've already been through eighth grade and I finished all my homework assignments then.

"Good," Patrick says. "Then you can do this real fast."

But that isn't true. Each time I have to read up on active and passive verbs or independent and dependent clauses before I can correct his sentences.

I know I'm making this homework business sound like a big deal. Those of you who don't have school-age children or those of you who have responsible kids (if there is such a kind) who don't need a drill sergeant to get them through the daily assignments must by happy that you can use your evenings to fill out your income tax returns instead doing long division problems.

Sometimes, though, homework can be fun. On a recent long car trip Patrick asked me to look over a descriptive speech he was to make about a classmate. First I corrected his spelling and made some grammatical changes. Then I saw a few points he could elaborate on.

I rearranged some of his paragraphs so the speech would have a better flow, then I suggested a few anecdotes about his friend to make the speech more interesting.

I was having a great time. Each new line inspired me to write something even more clever. I thought to myself, "I'm making this speech so wonderful I wish I could give it to Patrick's class."

Patrick must have read my mind because he said, "Mom, I thought you already finished eighth grade."

"Sure," I answered, "but my mother did all my fun assignments."

January 29, 1986

8 • HOOPLA AND HAPPY TIMES

Horan

All-Nighters Sleep Where They Fall

On Friday nights our family has open sleeping. No one is happy unless he or she has someone stay overnight or he or she is staying overnight at someone's house. A regular old evening at home with mom and dad is just about the most boring possible way to spend a Friday.

The request to have overnight guests on Friday begins on Monday. Usually, I don't answer one way or another in hopes the notion will pass as the week does.

Usually, it doesn't and on Thursday the hounding begins and my resistance ends. "Fine," I say with less and less sincerity as each request is made.

I don't know what other parents do for their children's overnight guests but I don't do anything especially for Patrick's buddies. I let them eat whatever is around and they always manage to find something. One morning I woke up and discovered they had made a bowl of cake mix batter and eaten it.

I never worry about where they all (Patrick never has just one guest) will sleep because they stay up all night. High school freshmen think 1 a.m. is the time to start a game of *Monopoly* or *Axis and Allies*.

The combination of game playing, TV watching, cake baking, and of course, telephoning takes until sunrise, when the guys collapse completely dressed including shoes in the nearest somewhat comfortable spot.

If I didn't have other plans for my basement family room floor on Saturdays, or if the mothers of the guests didn't have plans for their sons, I'd have several inert lumps residing there until midafternoon.

I try to generate some life by sending down the little kids or by turning on the vacuum cleaner.

One parenting skill I have acquired is: If I bribe the kids to do something, they have to pay up front. For example, if Patrick promises to clean my car in exchange for having friends over, the car has to be cleaned beforehand, because his good intentions become good for nothing after a good night with the good ol' boys.

On her last birthday Maureen held me to a three-year-old promise for a slumber party. The first birthday that she asked I said she was too young. The next year I said the baby was too young, he wasn't even born but was expected any minute. The next year I said I was too old. Finally, this year I gave in.

Colleen, the great entertainer, who loves to give parties, thinks the girls who come should stay over night afterwards. I say they should go home.

"When your Dad and I have friends over, at the end of the evening everyone goes home. They don't even think about staying overnight."

"That's because people your age don't stay overnight at people's houses. They have to go home and take care of their kids," Colleen answered.

"That's not the reason. People my age don't stay overnight because sleeping on the couch or the floor doesn't appeal to them when they could be sleeping comfortably at home in their own bed."

Most of the time the overnight guest is no problem. Occasionally, a younger one gets scared around midnight and wants to go home.

The problem I have is with my own kids. Where is everyone going to sleep so everyone is happy?

I tell them to just go to sleep and it won't matter that the guest is sleeping in Machaela's bed and Machaela has to sleep alone in Colleen's bed because Colleen is sleeping overnight at her friend's house.

This problem is eventually settled but first we have to have some tears and some pouting and some "No fair!" accusations.

Even my little guys have had their friend, Mark John, stay over. They think the big kids get to have guests so why shouldn't they?

Getting them to bed isn't a problem. It is the morning that comes too soon. They get up to watch Saturday cartoons just when Patrick and friends are going to bed.

I know this overnight ritual sounds crazy but I put up with it with one stipulation – No one sleeps in my bed!

March 4, 1987

Birthday Season Is a Happy Time of Hoopla

I just returned from taking John's birthday treat to school. He is seven years old today.

He had his birthday party last Saturday. We took a group roller skating and had a big time, so today is more of a low key celebration.

When I drove up to school, John was outside for lunch recess. I think he and his friends were getting ready to tease some girls, but when he saw my car he ran over to see me.

He looked so cute with the Happy Birthday sticker from his teacher on his school sweater. I patted him on the head and put my arm around him and asked if he was having a good birthday.

He looked like he was having fun. It made me feel good.

When I drove back home again my mind wandered back to the day he was born. I had a pleasant time reminiscing about that day and how happy we were.

John was a beautiful big baby with not an abundance of hair but an abundance of bright orange color in the hair he did have, and he was born with good health, which he continues to enjoy.

I remembered holding him in my arms. I loved doing that. I wondered if after school I could get him to sit on my lap.

I know that Patrick, my oldest, who just had his birthday, can't sit on my lap any more. Even though he started out as a real big baby I didn't expect him to grow up so fast, but he did anyway. That is why now I sit on his lap.

This is the birthday season at our house. We have five birthdays in one month's time. That is a lot of cake and ice cream. Hoopla is involved in all our occasions. So we have been busy planning and giving parties and cleaning up afterwards.

This doesn't give me much time to think about the actual birth day of the birthday person and how life has changed since. Each birthday of my children is important to the celebrant because it is another step in life's progression. But to me each child's birthday is the anniversary of a dramatic change in my life: a change that was immediately joyous and continues to be enriching, fulfilling and happy, sometimes infuriatingly so. The deep love and commitment to well-being that a parent develops for a child is a bond I hadn't thought about before my first child was born – although, I grew up as a child loved that way – and I didn't realize it could be continually duplicated with the birth of each succeeding child.

These are thoughts I should be having but it is hard because Maureen keeps interjecting her train of thought into mine. She wants me to quit philosophizing about motherhood and be a mother so we can plan her birthday party. At the moment she wants to discuss the invitations.

"I need to give them out at school tomorrow." she says

"Why don't I get them tomorrow while you're at school and you can give them out the next day?" I suggest.

"No, I want to go with you so you don't buy anything too babyish."

We've compromised by Maureen trusting my good taste and me buying the invitations today.

Pete's birthday will be another festivity. He has been practicing up for the gala event he is planning for when he turns four by blowing out the candles on everyone else's cake.

I've been trying to explain to him that he is only going to be 3 but he insists I'm wrong. So I've given up. You'll understand why if you have ever tried to change a 2-plus-year-old's mind.

The fifth birthday on the Cavanaugh celebration agenda is the one belonging to the Mom, the Boss, the Missus, or the Old Lady (You know whom I mean).

At this point in the 30 days of birthdays, I feel my day will give a new twist to the old saying "You are not getting older you are getting better." But in my case, after eating all the nut cups and leftover birthday cake, I think it should be, "I'm not getting older, just filling out and having fun!"

October 28, 1987

Birthday Luau at 'Waikiki Basement' Is Another Event That Got Out of Hand

Last fall, Colleen surveyed her friends. She presented four possibilities and each girl had to vote. The question posed was: For my 12th birthday should I have a Marilyn Monroe party, Hawaiian party, Fairy Princess party or pink party? The Hawaiian party was the overwhelming winner.

When Colleen told me the news I said something like, "Oh, that's nice."

At the time, I wasn't particularly interested in Colleen's birthday. I had to have birthdays for Patrick, Johnny, Maureen, Pete and even myself before it would be Colleen's turn, and I knew she would remind me. She did.

Preparations began in the grocery store. While I was in the produce department, Colleen wandered off. When she reappeared she told me she had been discussing Hawaiian flowers with a woman in the flower shop.

"They don't regularly carry the kind of flowers I want for the party but they can special-order them," Colleen told me.

"By all means," I said. "We'll have them flown in from the Islands if necessary."

Phone calls between Colleen and her friends made the plans increasingly more elaborate.

One night when we were driving out to see Halley's comet, Colleen told her friend who had come along, "We have everyone's spot for sleeping figured out."

"This is not going to be a sleepover!" I yelled from the front seat.

That was the extent of my involvement until two days before the party, when it became another one of those things I let get out of hand.

First, we had to clean the basement. Colleen understood this, but her idea of clean and mine aren't the same. She wanted to clear a path and hang decorations. I suggested a more thorough job.

Colleen wanted the upstairs to be California and the basement to be Waikiki Beach. We hung up an "aloha" banner, a fish windsock and a hammock full of dolls dressed in bathing suits. One of her friends whose parents had been to Hawaii lent her some authentic decorations to put on the food table. I bought some paper umbrellas to place in the tropical drinks and the food, a couple pineapples, and figures of a hula girl and a guy on a surfboard.

Next came planning the entertainment. Colleen decided on a Hula-Hoop contest, a limbo contest, Hula dancing with the dancers taking turns wearing Colleen's grass skirt, a tropical drink-making event, a Hawaiian Luau with all the trimmings except the roast pig, a movie to watch on the video recorder and going out for pizza.

I agreed to everything except the drink-making, because it sounded too messy, and the pizza outing, because it seemed unnecessary.

The day of the party I shopped for Hula-Hoops and a limbo record. Three sales people helped me search the music store, but we couldn't come up with any version of the limbo. I decided we'd have to improvise – I still had to shop for the luau.

By the time the three little guys and I got home from shopping, the big kids were home from school and ready to go Hawaiian. My disposition was still on the mainland.

Once I got out the blender to start mixing the banana-raspberry slush, which I had to make with strawberries and no orange juice (I forgot to get raspberries and orange juice at the store), my spirits picked right up.

At 7 p.m. when the guests arrived in their Hawaiian outfits, the basement looked as close to a Hawaiian beach as a basement in Omaha, Nebraska, can in January. At the end of the evening when the guests indicated they had a great time, Colleen said, "This has been the best party I've ever had. I bet I'll always remember it."

As I surveyed the damage on Waikiki Beach I said, "I'm so glad, because I don't think I'll be ready for another one until your wedding reception."

February 12, 1986

Party a Great Excuse for Grand Illusions

Have you ever said, "We are just going to have a few people over?"

I know I have and we both know we were lying.

Nobody "just has a few friends over." The part about the friends is true. They actually come, and hopefully everyone has a good time. The lie is in saying "just."

There is nothing just (as in simple as opposed to right and fair) in waging war against dirt and disorder in your home. It is a big job to try to fool your guests into thinking you always live graciously, elegantly, and, most of all, neatly. Whenever I have a party, big or small, I have a mission to create the illusion of a House Beautiful and it is never just "just."

Are you guilty of going to a party at someone's home thinking, "Gee, it would be great to live here, everything is so neat and clean. All they probably had to do to get ready was fluff the pillows, throw on a tablecloth, stick some flowers in a vase, and light the candles."

It is fine to think that, because that is what the hosts want you to believe even if they were out of breath when they answered the door.

Don't try to visualize how things looked a few hours earlier. Don't wonder:

-Where they stashed all the newspapers that were piled up;

-What they did with the junk stacked up on the kitchen counters;

-How they keep those knick knacks on the coffee table from getting broken;

-Do they always have those fancy handtowels in the bathroom folded like origami?

Supposedly the key to a successful party is to make it look effortless. I once read an article about party planning including a preparation timetable. The last half hour before the party begins you are supposed to have everything ready, including yourself. Then you and your spouse can spend a few moments relaxing and catching your breath in front of the fire.

I've never managed to do this except when our guests are late. If they are even five minutes early, prospects are good for finding me in hair curlers and sweatsuit on my hands and knees washing the floor.

Usually, the first doorbell ring is my cue to run upstairs and get gorgeous. What's good about this initial lack of attention is that guests get to browse around the house drinking in the illusion I busted a gasket to create.

These house cleaning details are fresh in my mind because I just had a party. Things looked great around here. Too bad it doesn't last.

A party is good incentive to do stuff that needs doing but never gets done. There are the big preparations like gutting the kitchen and adding a room, which I did last year before we had a graduation party for John's sister.

For the recent event I didn't get quite so carried away, although I removed an ugly light fixture, had a sofa re-upholstered, had new pillows and table skirt made, and cleaned, cleaned, and cleaned. I started out organizing, and ended up stuffing and throwing things, mostly into the garage.

It would be easier to get ready if I had some cooperation from my offspring, but they don't understand why they have to pick up their bedrooms if we are having guests in the dining room, or why they have to clean the basement when no one will go down there.

"Because I want it cleaned," I answer. "I can't have people in a clean house with a dirty basement. That is like getting dressed in clean clothes after taking a shower and putting dirty socks back on."

Having the house bordering on perfection is my dream for entertaining. Not surprisingly, it doesn't occur. What is surprising is what gets accomplished when party time is minutes away. A couple hours of sorting and organizing work is scooped in a couple of seconds into grocery bags and hustled into hiding. Lace doilies and bouquets of flowers camouflage banged up tables. Furniture is rearranged to make it more presentable, lights are dimmed so the dirty windows aren't so obvious and a can of leftover paint and a q-tip are used to touch up all the nicks on the walls.

Then we are as ready for the festivities as we'll ever be.

March 22, 1988

Job of Eating Leftovers Falls to the Party Hostess

A fun part of having a party is later, when only a few guests remain. You relax, take off your shoes, hash over what happened and eat the leftovers.

We just had a brunch and it was great fun, with one exception. The leftover guests said they were too full to eat the leftovers, which left the whole task up to me.

Unfortunately, this is not an insurmountable job. My mouth is more than willing, even eager, to eat anything – rich, delicious, and usually forbidden – it can sink its teeth into.

My hips have another reaction, usually involving expansion.

Several friends offered to bring "something" for the brunch, so we had a magnificent display of cakes, coffee cakes and other sweets. As the guests circled the buffet table, I encouraged them to treat their palates luxuriously and try all the offerings at least once.

After everyone had been fed, I noticed the bounty was still bountiful, so I began pressing guests to make repeat visits.

Despite my urgings, the table still had a million-calorie price tag, so I began pushing food on people as they departed. But my designated receivers were reluctant.

"All these kids will take care of what's left," one said.

This is a logical assumption, except my kids never eat good homemade pastries. If the table were laden with Ho-Ho's and Twinkies, I'm sure there would have been nothing left to give away.

"I don't need it," was the other response.

"Neither do I," I would say. "So give it to your bus driver or cab driver . . . Take it into work tomorrow . . . Have your neighbors in for coffee . . . Have your son take it to Cub Scouts . . . Freeze it and bring it back next time we have a party."

Despite all these attempts, the inevitable happened. I was left with too many unavoidably good things to eat.

When this happens, there are a couple courses of action.

At one extreme is the sensible approach of wrapping all the leftovers for the freezer and saying, "I've had enough sweets for one day."

Of course, this involves self-control and since I have none, I usually follow the course that involves stuffing myself.

That's what I did after the brunch. After all, I couldn't let all that good cooking go to waste. But when I went to bed feeling like a filled kolache, I told myself, "Tomorrow I'm not going to touch any of that stuff. I'll save some for the kids and give the rest away."

I woke up with that resolve, and it lasted until I got downstairs and came face to face with a plate of homemade sweet rolls.

Before I knew it, I was off and eating, climbing that mountain of desserts, eating them just because they were there.

What's the key to avoiding these after-party leftover benders? I could have another party immediately for some big eaters, or I could serve less. But I never will, because even when I have too much food I worry about having enough.

The only good answer is for all the food to become low-calorie as soon as the party ends. I wonder how I could do that?

April 16, 1986

Saying 'I Do' Is the Easy Part

It used to be that heading a young woman's list in planning a wedding was finding Mr. Right. I'm not sure it is anymore.

The time necessary for choosing the china, deciding on the flowers, planning the table decorations, finding the caterer, reserving the church and picking a place for the reception seems to diminish the importance of the lifelong decision you make when you choose a spouse.

Horan

Until recently, I had no idea that planning a wedding could be such a big deal. My wedding was quite a while ago, so either I had forgotten what getting married entailed or I was too naive or maybe too blinded by love to notice.

It's not so any longer. My sister's wedding was last month, John's sister's is this month, and my college-girl helper's is next month.

It seems as if all my conversations revolve around weddings. I've been shuffling information from bride to bride.

Depending on whom I'm talking to I'll say, "Kerry is going to spray her flower girl's basket white." "Mary Pat's cake top was made out of flowers." "Marg wants all the nieces to carry baskets of flowers."

All the brides are trying to figure out how to achieve the overall effect they have dreamed their wedding would have, and I've been busy giving them, free of charge of course, my opinion.

I tell them "How I like," which is what the florist in Germany – where I was married – told me.

He said, "How I like, one bouquet on one side of the altar," as he demonstrated by running back and forth through his shop, "and one bouquet over there." It didn't seem to matter to him that I didn't want red gladiolus on the altar at my wedding since "how he like" was "what I got."

My children have become intrigued with the wedding shower ritual. They can't understand how there can be so many different types of showers.

I flew back to my hometown for two showers for my sister, Mary Pat. One was a luncheon given at a restaurant. We gave what Machaela called a private shower for Kerry, where she received pretty nighties and lingerie for her trousseau.

The next week, the girls and I went to a housewares shower at Grandma's house for her good friend's daughter. Many of the guests received door prizes. Last week there was a shower in the church hall for Marg. The gifts were mostly for the kitchen or bath, and there was a clothes pin drawing for door prizes.

What was most remarkable about that shower, according to Machaela, was that Johnny and Mike attended. "Boys at a shower? Won't everyone think that's funny."

She and Maureen were really confused the next night when there was a couples shower for Marg and her "intended," Steve. I was overwhelmed with questions.

"Will Steve be the only boy there?" "Is Dad going to go?" "Do grooms have showers, too, where everyone gives them nighties and underwear presents?"

Getting married is a process often lamented by the parties involved. But it acts as a test of steadfast love.

If the bride, groom and their parents weather the prenuptial storms reasonably unscathed (emotionally, at least – it would be impossible not to suffer monetarily), making the marriage work should seem easy.

I'm not at all worried about the times when I will have to plan our daughters' weddings. I know everything will go beautifully, just as long as we do it "How I like."

July 3, 1985

Democracy's Birthday Deserves All the Hoopla

The Fourth of July is my favorite holiday, after Christmas and Thanksgiving. It's always such a fun day.

Like many Americans, I have Norman Rockwell-esque memories of the Fourths of my childhood. When I was young, my dad's sister, Aunt Liz, had the Fourth of July party in her back yard. It was always a big deal with lots of people.

The yard was decorated with colorful Japanese lanterns, tables were set up all over the lawn, and in the garage was the bar where the adults clustered.

That spot never interested me. My favorite spot was in the basement because it had an old-fashioned (even then) soft drink cooler, filled to overflowing with bottles of Coca-Cola. They were for all my brothers, sisters and cousins to drink, and we could have as much as we wanted.

On the day of the party, my mother would get all of us (I am one of eight children) festively outfitted by dressing us in matching red, white and blue clothes. We all had to look perfect so the relatives would make the appropriate comments on how cute we were.

We always had corn on the cob. Back in the old days – the early 1950's – it was a big treat to have corn so early in the summer. Every year, my grandfather arranged to have it sent in from Texas.

Of course, I didn't know that, I just enjoyed eating the corn after my dad had cooked it in the husks over an open fire.

One year, my sister Bonnie, who was a big corn eater, lost two baby teeth while she was eating an ear. She collected 50-cent pieces from the aunts and uncles, which really made me mad.

Most of my other memories of these parties come from the home movies my dad took. One time he told my grandma that he wanted to get some footage of her and my grandpa with all the grandchildren. She thought he was going to take a picture, so she tried to get everyone to stand still. The result is a funny scene with

Grandma Nellie and Grandpa John posing for the camera and 25 to 30 grandchildren, drinking our bottles of pop, running all around them.

For the last several years, we have celebrated our nation's independence with family and friends at home. The day begins with a flag ceremony and a neighborhood parade and then there's badminton, Frisbee throwing, dancing, card playing, cooking out, eating and more eating. It is usually the kind of day that goes on and on until everyone is exhausted, stuffed and dirty.

We never need to go anywhere to watch a professional fireworks display because John, Patrick and my brother-in-law, Mike, get carried away with attempts to noisily illuminate our front yard.

My Fourth of July celebrations of 30-plus years ago as a child in suburban Chicago and the ones I now enjoy in our back yard in Omaha have one important detail in common. They have been fun.

And if we would all pause this Independence Day over a slice of watermelon, everyone would certainly agree that this much hoopla is appropriate to celebrate the formation of a democracy more than 200 years ago that in 1986 is still steadfast in its belief that people should forever enjoy freedom, opportunity and hope for the future.

July 2, 1986

Able-Bodied Dancers Toss the Salad, Shake Their Tail Feathers

My side hurts. Actually, I hurt all over. These sore muscles are ones I haven't used in a while but I really used them yesterday.

We had a big group over for a cookout and to see some friends visiting from out of town. I enlisted some able bodies (as it turned out, some able dancers) to help me in the kitchen.

As we started tossing the salad and getting out the silverware, plates, and napkins, Colleen said, "We need some music." She put on a Supremes tape and before Diana Ross sang the second "Baby Love, I Need Your love" we were rocking and rolling around the refrigerator.

Cousin Molly then fast forwarded the tape to "Stop In The Name of Love" so she, Colleen, and Andrea could do their "Supremes on stage" performance.

This song was followed by another tune, and the strength of the kitchen floor was tested when we all tried to out wiggle each other.

I was partners with Molly who then cut in on her mother, Pat, who was peeling an avocado, slicing mushrooms and shaking her tail feathers all at once.

Then I was partners with Johnny, Mike, a late arriving guest and then her husband. And finally I was dancing with a pot holder (by the way, I was drinking ice water.)

When we had exhausted the Sixties sound, another guest ran to the car to get her Pointer Sisters tape and we continued the impromptu sock hop (although, most of us were barefooted and in bathing suits, it is a good thing no one was there with a camera) until the bratwursts and sausages were grilled.

As you can tell, I'm a kitchen dancer, also a laundry room dancer, and a car dancer. Colleen gave me the Supremes tape for my car so I could be-bop through traffic.

Sometimes I even like to dance in the grocery store. I think my visiting niece, Julie, was a bit startled when I started to tango with her in the cereal aisle to the tune of Hernando's Hideaway but she didn't pretend that she didn't know me. She figured she was a long way from home and no one knew her.

It doesn't seem like I get to dance much on occasions when dancing is customarily done, such as at weddings or dinner dances. I have trouble finding a dancing partner. If I use the proper persuasion I can get the husband on the dance floor for a spin or two.

What's the proper persuasion? Usually I say something like, "You can't leave here and go home and get comfortable until we've been on the dance floor. Standing at the floor's edge chatting with another balking husband doesn't count."

This tactic works once in a while if I'm lucky. If any of my kids are at the party I can dance every dance. They all love to dance – even baby Matthew. He was just bouncing up and down to the music on a T.V. commercial.

Two-year-old Pete is another guy who's got the beat. The other day in church he was sitting on the floor fiddling with the kneeler when the choir began singing "Holy, Holy, Holy" and he stood up, took my hands and said, "Let's dance." That was one of the few times I've been inclined to decline a dance invitation.

Maureen and Machaela have put their lives to music. They frequently dress in old dance recital costumes and put on dance performances for me and anyone else they can get to watch. Maureen was really in her element when we were doing the remodeling and the scaffolding was set up in the new room.

By day the carpenters pounded on it and by night Maureen performed on it. She used a hairbrush for a microphone and sang, danced, wiggled, and wondered if Patrick could videotape her and send the tape to MTV.

After last night's kitchen production, I'm wondering if maybe we could do a mother-daughter act.

July 1, 1987

. . . .

She Must Be a Saint to Organize a Haunted House

"Did you know that it takes several miracles to be canonized a saint?" Colleen asked the other day as I was doing some penance at the kitchen sink.

"Yes, I've heard that," I answered, adding, "After the past weekend I feel assured I've reached my quota and I'm a sure pick for canonization."

"I doubt making a haunted house in the garage qualifies as performing a miracle," Colleen replied.

"Want to bet?"

"Well, the miracle has to be documented."

"That's why I'm writing about it. After I've gone to that big costume party in the sky, the canonization team can dig this column out, nod their heads in agreement, and then immediately hustle me right up next to the Archangel."

John celebrated his 8th birthday last weekend with a haunted house party. It was a big success because it was such a nightmare.

It wasn't even his fault.

As his birthday approached he began discussing party ideas. Most of them I vetoed because I thought there would be too much commotion. I thought he should have his party at home. It would be more fun, more memorable, and – as it turned out – more expensive and more of a mess.

I remembered Patrick's 8th birthday, which was a lot of fun, and I thought it would be nice if John had a similar party 8 years later. What I failed to remember was we had to have Patrick's party outside because we had just moved into our house, and all the floors were being refinished and we couldn't walk on them.

John said he'd have his party at home if he could have a haunted house party. I agreed to this.

He wanted to have it in the basement. I vetoed that idea and said the garage would be the site. He pouted. I was firm. I won on this point. It turned out to be the only point I did win.

Once we settled on the location, date and time, we went to a party goods store with a whole entourage of young celebrants all very eager to purchase party wares. Everything in the store was appealing from the black bat hanging on a string to a tube of slime.

However, there were no invitations John felt were appropriate.

"Everyone will think these are stupid." he said. This meant we had to go on another invitation buying outing the next day. Once again I was well accompanied, no one wanted to miss another fun time. Still we couldn't find invitations John liked.

Next, I put my big kids plus all their friends on notice that I expected their help with a capital "H." I needed ideas for the haunted house, I needed manpower to put it all together, and I needed bodies to run it during the party. Their response lacked the enthusiasm necessary to carry this off: "Mom, why do you always get such dumb ideas?"

After the invitations were finally delivered, John, Machaela and Maureen began to fight about how things should be done. Skirmishes erupted every half hour right up to and through the party.

One especially inflammatory moment occurred when Machaela discovered that John had put fake blood on her Cabbage Patch doll, Mort Timmy, who has resided on the bottom of the toy cabinet never seeing the light of day for at least two years.

She was quite upset and when she said she was going to kill John I feared the next blood I'd see would not be fake.

However, that incident passed, as did John's fits about the haunted house not being scary enough and no one letting him help, that he wasn't coming to the party and that everything looked dumb.

The night before the party, when nobody had done anything to get the haunted house assembled except fight, I realized I had to intervene. I started giving orders and rummaging through closets for props.

As things got messier and messier and I became more unglued, I realized the haunted house was a disaster.

So I turned out the lights, ducked when the glow-in-dark skeleton flew in front of me, slid down the slide through a curtain made from a grass skirt into a gravel graveyard assembled on a tablecloth, crawled through a cardboard box somebody was shaking and rattling and then threw myself on the couch brought up from the basement and started screaming.

Suddenly, I thought: This is a miracle. It's a success. Happy Halloween!

October 25, 1988

Over the River and Through the Years

The air in late November is great. It is the air of anticipation.

The Wednesday before Thanksgiving is a day I love for that reason. It is an over the river and through the woods kind of day. A day of arrivals of family and friends who are visiting or a day of departures to become the visitor.

It is the day for going to the airport, train depot or bus station or watching for a car with outstate or out-of-state license plates to pull in the drive.

It is important on this day to go the grocery store, the flower shop, and to buy the New York or California (it should be American) wine to compliment the turkey.

Then when Thanksgiving day arrives, so many happy things happen: The eating, the gathering of family and friends, the dishwashing, the giving of thanks, football, more eating, and more dishwashing are some of them.

We usually celebrate Thanksgiving with all the Omaha Cavanaughs unless we decide to travel to Illinois to see the Barretts. We decide at whose house we will celebrate Thanksgiving during one of the November birthday parties.

Last year we had it at our house and it was one of my favorite Thanksgivings. We had lots of people, lots of food, lots of fun and now we have lots of warm memories.

All the family was here and everyone had someone extra visiting from out of town to bring along. We set up tables all over the place.

Grandma Cavanaugh and Aunt Cathie brought over their silver place settings and extra folding chairs. I made table cloths and every one cooked.

John and I put the turkey in the oven, peeled potatoes, and I made the cranberry salad I like and all the trimmings were fixed by our guest chefs.

To make table conversation interesting and to give guests who don't regularly have the opportunity to dine next to a small person a chance to do so (if they wanted to or not) Machaela devised a seating plan. She put a number at each place, then passed around a dish of numbers for everyone to choose from and then match up with the place setting.

This system worked pretty well once everyone figured out that there was no system. After they found their numbers, which were the size of a piece of confetti, it was quickly apparent that there was no numerical order.

When I reminisce about our past Thanksgivings, it seems they all run together like the turkey gravy into the Jell-o mold on a crowded dinner plate. But this sameness makes it a tradition – one of elevated noise level and ongoing activity – but nevertheless a tradition, and I like it that way.

After the big meal is over we always wait before we take orders for pie. Every year Grandma Cavanaugh is on pie detail. Since the ability to get a pie crust off the rolling pin into the pie tin is a talent I don't have, I am always impressed when my Omaha mom shows up with seven pies: two apple, two pumpkin, two cherry, and one mincemeat. She explains that once you get started making pies you may as well keep going.

As the day unfolds, the dessert and coffee is served, and things liven up. Children run through the house, conversation groups spread out about the family room and kitchen, some people go outside for fresh air and to toss the football, others stay inside to watch football on TV. Just as a lull is approaching, late arriving guests appear, pumping new life into the party.

Each year I tell my children to think of things they are especially thankful for this year. I suggest the blessings of being born and living in America. They agree that is a good deal, but more important they are thankful for not losing all the soccer games, for toys, for finally learning the seven times tables, for a new jean jacket, and for friends who are finally old enough to drive.

That is okay because they are all things that are part of the bountiful life we celebrate on Thanksgiving.

November 25, 1987

Joy to the World! Family Photo Passes Muster for Christmas Card

My hands trembled as I opened the envelope.

Anticipation had been building as I retrieved the claim slip from my coat pocket, as the salesperson totaled my bill and as I wrote out the check. Now I was sitting in the car in the grocery store parking lot getting ready to look at the pictures. I took a deep breath.

What's wrong with me? Don't I have something more important to sweat over than pictures?

No, especially at this time of year. The pictures were of our family, taken in hopes of using one for our 1985 Christmas card. If you had been here Sunday afternoon for our photo session, you would understand my nervousness.

Each year we try to do a picture Christmas card. We used to take the picture on Thanksgiving, but as our family grew I realized that I couldn't stuff a turkey and curl my daughters' hair at the same time, so now we do the picture the Sunday before. It's a major effort.

Every year we receive similar picture cards from friends and relatives. Often the pictures are casual snapshots taken outside on a patio or on a vacation trip when everyone looks relaxed and natural.

I wish we could get a picture like that, but it never works. Instead, I spend a month getting ready: figuring out what everyone is going to wear; choosing a time to take the picture; getting everyone cleaned up, dressed up and primped up. Then I expect them to pose relaxed and natural.

Amazingly, every year we manage to get a picture. Last year we received a note from an out-of-town friend complimenting us on our card and questioning the tranquility the picture suggests.

"Your picture cards are great," she wrote, "but wouldn't it be more honest if you would accompany the posed photo with some shots of your crew getting ready for the picture?"

"Good point," I thought. "But sometimes delusion is better." It might diminish the effect to send out wishes for peace on earth and good will toward men with pictures of me wearing John's bathrobe, curling iron in one hand and a bottle of shoe polish in the other, screeching orders to Patrick to put on a decent pair of pants and to Colleen to get her nail polish away from the baby before he gets it all over his good outfit.

John does take some "before" shots of the kids. This year we have several pictures of the girls flopped down on the couch getting their clothes wrinkled and their hair messed up, of Mike lying on the floor crying and of Pete trying to chew on Patrick's nose.

There are none of Johnny and me because we were still upstairs. I was in the bathroom trying to make my hair grow; my new haircut made me look like Buster Brown. Johnny had spilled apple juice on his lap and wanted to change his pants. Since that would disturb the family color scheme, I rinsed the pants and put them in the dryer.

John may have considered capturing these tender moments on film, but his good manners – or maybe good sense – prevented him from becoming the victim of my lost composure.

Finally, when we were all ready and seated on the living room sofa, I breathed a sigh of relief. Now all I had to worry about was: Is the film in the camera the right speed? Is the light meter set correctly? Will the flash go off? Can John set the camera's automatic timer and get seated before the timer goes off?

After all this, you are wondering, did the pictures turn out? Yes, they are fine.

What if the pictures hadn't turned out? They still would be fine. We wouldn't take them again because there's something unnatural about trying to take a picture of your family looking natural.

November 27, 1985

Magic Sets Today Apart from Rest of the Year

This is my favorite day of the year. It's a day of magic.

Everything looks different today from any other day of the year. All the regular things like the street in front of our house, the gas stations on the corners, the stoplights and parking lots seem different and special somehow.

Those things don't really look different, they aren't even decorated for the holidays; they just seem different.

I've always felt this way on Christmas Eve, but my most magical memory was one Christmas Eve when I was about 7 or 8 years old.

I was in the bedroom that I shared with my sisters. We were supposed to be asleep, but we were too excited to sleep. Suddenly, my brother John, who was the oldest, ran into our room and said, "You better get to sleep. He's coming. He won't stop if you are still awake, and I just heard him over at the Sorensens (our neighbors)."

Without thinking of the risk, we all ran to the window, and a couple seconds later I saw Santa and his reindeer fly across our front lawn. And then just as quickly, I jumped back into bed.

It was probably the most exciting thing that ever happened to me. It is something that can happen only on a magical night such as this.

There are so many things to do to make Christmas a joyous occasion. The shopping is the most nerve wracking. Right now I feel like taking a vow never to enter another store.

Yet exchanging gifts is part of Christmas. It is important to remember in some way all those who have extended kindness to us throughout the year, to share some of our abundance with someone less blessed than ourselves and, of course, to do what we can to make this a bountiful holiday for our own families.

It is particularly important not to go overboard on that last one, but we always do.

I enjoy seeing how people deck their homes, churches and businesses. We decorate inside the house with poinsettias, evergreens, red bows and a tree covered with ornaments collected over the years. Hung on the fireplace is an assortment of Christmas stockings starting with the ones John and I bought in Germany for our first Christmas together and ending with the Baby's First Christmas sock for Matthew.

Depending on the weather, we decorate the outside of the house with colored lights and wreaths. I always have more grandiose plans for decorating than ever get carried out.

We drive past homes that are elaborately decorated. I use the excuse that the kids enjoy seeing the lights and decorations, but I enjoy it as much as and sometimes even more than they do.

The music of Christmas has the ability to immediately create a holiday mood, with the exception of "Grandma got Run Over by a Reindeer," which is ridiculous. I look forward to singing my favorites, "O Come All Ye Faithful" and "Joy to the World" at the Christmas Eve children's Mass.

The foods at all the holiday occasions are a sweet lover's (which I am) dream come true. Sampling all the cookies I brought home from the cookie exchanges was my Christmas present for my tastebuds.

Do you suppose that Jesus had any idea when he was born in Bethlehem that so many generations after we'd make such elaborate preparations for the celebration of his birth?

I'm sure the Christ Child would be pleased to know that once all the presents are wrapped, the lights are strung, the cookies are baked, before the family is gathered and when the house is quiet, most of us take a moment to look outside, or maybe inside ourselves, and find the magic of the "The First Noel." That's why I love Christmas.

December 24, 1986

9 • BELL BOTTOMS WILL BE BACK

Tons of Sisters, and Stuff Like That

A boy we know has no brother but says he has "tons of sisters."

His mother, when complimented on her new dress, answered, "Thank you, I like it too, but I'm afraid I'll see myself coming and going. There were tons of them on the rack in the store."

When asked about a party, Colleen said, "They had tons of pizza and tons of pop."

When asked if I argued with the kids over doing the dishes, I used to say "Sure, tons of times." But not any more.

"Tons" has been getting a verbal workout. When I hear that expression, I imagine whatever there are tons of, such as a huge pile of sisters or a mountain of dresses.

A ton is 2,000 pounds. When people say they have tons of sisters or pop or pizza, they are merely exaggerating. When people say tons of times, they are causing confusion because time can't be measured in pounds – unless you are talking about time that weighs heavily on your hands.

I had a couple of "ton" sayings. When I had a lot of laundry, I'd say "I have a ton of laundry." On days the dirty clothes were really piling up, I'd say "I have 10 tons of laundry."

When I had too much to eat and felt my waistline expanding I'd say "I feel like Two-Ton Baker."

Those sayings fit the circumstances. That was before the tons overdose, before tons of folks were filling tons of sentences with the word tons.

From now on, instead of saying I have tons of work to do I'll say "I have work to do and stuff like that." An aura of mystery will be added to my life.

After hearing someone say, "I have to go to the gas station, the dentist and stuff like that," I always wonder about the "stuff like that." My curiosity goes on overload trying to decide if the "stuff like that" is more like the gas station or the dentist.

I never do "stuff like that" because my kids are always asking me, "Are you going to take me shopping or what? Are you going to make dinner or what?" And I'm trying to figure out the "or what."

Do they mean, "Are you going to take me shopping or enjoy the luxury of going alone?" Or do they mean, "Are you going to fix dinner or do you want me to do it while you lie down on the couch?"

I doubt it. I think they mean "Are you going to make dinner or talk on the telephone all night?" Or, "Are you taking me shopping or are you going alone and get all the wrong stuff?"

Of course, it would be difficult to get the wrong "stuff" because everything is stuff. No one runs back upstairs to get their gym clothes. They go after their stuff. When I asked Patrick what he has for homework, he always answers "stuff" instead of math or social studies.

The stuff I use to wash my hair is a lot cheaper than the stuff my hairdresser tells me to use. The stuff on television is often similar to the stuff found in the trash can. The stuff we are having for dinner is leftover from the stuff we had last night.

So you don't get mixed up, I had better clarify. Although there is plenty of stuff around and lots of stuff to do, none of this is "stuff like that."

Straightening out the spoken word would take tons of work, I could try to and stuff like that, but do you think it's a good idea or what?

October 30, 1985

· ·

Now That's Customer Service

One of the first questions asked me when I returned to Omaha after living for four years in Washington, D.C. was "What do you like most about being back?"

Invariably, I'd answer "grocery shopping." I'd say it to be funny (I'm always so clever), but it is also true.

Grocery shopping, which is not my favorite pastime, is almost bearable in the heartland.

In the nation's capital – even in the suburbs – it isn't because employees don't carry your groceries to your car. You either do it yourself or push your cart into a line, take a number, and then drive your car up so an attendant can load the groceries.

That is not a bad system, it just isn't as quick and convenient as having someone accompany your loaded cart to the car. That is service.

I like service. Not bowing and scraping service or room service in a swank hotel – although that is nice to dream about – but genuine, honest service that says, "I like having your business and I want to satisfy you."

The kind of service that makes it a little easier to lower the balance in the checkbook or raise the balance on the credit card.

I shop at Baker's Grocery store at 84th and Frederick Square where I get that kind of treatment. I like it, appreciate it and keep going back for it.

I don't just get groceries there. I also cash checks, sometimes eat lunch in the restaurant, buy postage stamps, and drop off film to be developed.

A recent episode involving the processing of photo reprints is what inspired this column. Don't you think if someone does something extra he should be acknowledged?

One of the grocery managers, whose name is Bob Trant, really helped me out. It didn't involve a life-or-death issue, but one that was important to me.

I was having a large number of 35mm pictures reprinted for my Christmas card. I called around town to check prices and determined that Baker's offered the best special, but the price didn't take effect for a few days.

I talked to Bob and he assured me that I could have the special price. He alerted the employees at the courtesy desk to write up my order when I brought in the negatives.

So we were all set. Except over the weekend I realized I miscounted and really needed many more than I already ordered.

I called Baker's and they called the photo processing people who said it was too late to add on to the order. I'd have to reorder the extras.

But the photo processor had my negative, and by the time the first batch was completed, time would be running out for my pre-Christmas mailing if we had to wait for the reorder to be completed.

This is when Bob got in the act.

He called back and forth between the processing plant and me, he talked to me about the progress when I was in the store which is all the time, and finally we figured out a solution. The processor, I should add, was trying very hard to help us out at the busiest time of year.

I began to feel that getting my picture reprinted was Bob's full time job. Except I knew better, because every time I saw him he was busy handling many other things.

Unfortunately, things didn't pan out as we planned.

The day the reprints came in one of the young women at the customer service desk immediately called me so I could come to the store to get them and remake the order for the additional number. When I arrived I discovered that the wrong negative had been reprinted and reprinted and reprinted 500 times (we have lots of relatives).

Bob came through once again. It was 4:50 p.m. He left the meeting he was attending to come to the front desk. He called the photo processing plant, explained what had happened. And then because the plant closed at 5 p.m. he hand delivered my negative. He said the plant was on his way home – sort of.

Anyway, to sum up a long story the whole order was completed at 1 p.m. the next day.

When I thanked Bob for all the extra effort he and the staff at Bakers made for me he said simply, "I'm glad we could get it done for you. That's why we are here."

I like that attitude.

January 6, 1988

I'd Tip My Hat To You, But . . .

Last winter when Patrick and John returned home from a ski trip, they had gifts for all of us. Mine was a pink corduroy baseball cap with the resort's name embroidered on it.

"This is cute," I said.

"Will you wear it?" Patrick asked.

"Where would I wear it?"

"Skiing," John answered.

"It doesn't cover my ears," I told them. "The only reason I wear a hat is to keep my ears warm. If it is warm enough out to go hatless I do, because hats flatten my hair."

But that was then and this is now. I've come to my senses, or should I say my sinuses, and realized if I want to be cool, which of course I do, I'll have to wear a hat: not a pillbox, a Panama or a floppy brimmed one, but a baseball cap with something written above the bill.

Have you noticed that some kids are never without a hat? The ones who come to our house have their heads topped and, for sure, we only have the coolest of the cool hanging out here (one of them forced me to say that).

They wear hats to school, and they'd wear them in the classroom if it were allowed. They wear them for movies, games, parties, shopping and hanging around the house.

I asked Patrick's buddy Joey why he always has on a hat. He said, "Because I like to wear a hat. You can quote me on that."

It used to be that only guys with balding heads wore a hat outdoors, to prevent a sunburned scalp. When I was a kid, if you wore a hat in the house it was speculated that you would become one of the permanently hatted because your hair would fall out.

Farmers were among the initiators of this baseball-style cap craze, because for years they have worn the caps given to them by the feed and seed companies where they did business. Now every team for every sport sells caps as souvenirs. Every school, beer and scenic spot has a hat with its design emblazoned across it, and I think we have at least one of each type.

Since I am always seeking ways to enhance my image, I decided to don a hat. I chose a Chicago Cubs hat purchased by Maureen when her dad took her to a genuine Cubs game. When I arrived at my friend's house wearing the hat, no one said anything or even seemed to notice. This continued until I couldn't stand it any longer.

"You haven't said anything about my hat."

"I was wondering if you were wearing it because something was wrong with your hair," my friend answered.

I think what she meant to say was, "You are cool, cool, cool!"

Later that night when John and I walked to return a videocassette, I wore the hat to check the reaction of the public. Would they realize I was cool now? Apparently not. No one noticed me except a guy who yelled out of his car window that the Mets beat the Cubs 23 to 10. Darn, I thought. I should have worn the Mets hat.

Just because you wear a hat doesn't necessarily mean you are rooting for that team or have an affection for that place. We have hats for the Red Sox, White Sox, Mets, Cubs and two College World Series. We also play no favorites in wearing hats from colleges, vacation spots or social events.

It just means someone in our family was there and brought back a hat, or someone wore the hat to our house and forgot it. Just as my pink corduroy hat no longer lives here – it only comes to visit on the head of Patrick's buddy, Tom.

He won't let me have it back, but that's OK. I know he is wearing it because he wants to be like me, now that I'm cool.

September 2, 1987

This He-Man Is a Hero a Mother Could Love

At the part of the Mass when the priest holds up the host and says, "By the power of the Holy Spirit," I hold my breath.

It is inevitable that one of my children will respond with, "By the power of Greyskull, I have the power."

If you don't know what I'm talking about, you're not up to date with kid-video. Greyskull is the castle where Prince Adam lives. He transforms into the hero, He-Man (be sure to accent "he"), by raising his sword and proclaiming, "by the power of Greyskull, I have the power."

Horan

"He-Man – Masters of the Universe," a weekday afternoon cartoon show, is all the rage with the preschool crowd, as well as the after-school crowd.

I have never given the show my complete attention. All my little friends are so involved in He-Man's adventures that, when he's on, I find myself in the luxurious position to do something uninterrupted.

After several months of watching glimpses of the action and of hearing my children talk, I understand the show to be set on the legendary planet of Eternia. Prince Adam becomes He-Man to stop Skeletor and Evil-Lyn (the bad guys, in case you didn't guess it) from taking over Eternia.

Interest in He-Man does not end when the half hour show does. As a matter of fact, it never seems to end. When the He-Man fans are not watching He-Man on television, they are playing He-Man. If they are not playing He-Man, they are at least dressing as He-Man.

For Christmas, 4-year-old John received He-Man's sword, shield and cuffs. The sword fell apart, which is convenient, because it is now two swords which John and 2-year-old Mike insist on wearing stuck down the back of their shirts.

I didn't understand this style, but after Mike kept giving me the sword and saying "He-Man" (I think those were his first words) it occurred to me that Prince Adam must wear it that way.

Mike also runs around the house with his arm extended, wearing a mitten on his hand. Someone asked me whether he was pretending to be Michael Jackson. I said I doubted it because he was growling.

The older kids tell me Mike is acting like Clawful, an evil lobster who is on Skeletor's side.

In addition to the He-Man armor, there is a whole array of 5 1/2-inch figures depicting the various Masters of the Universe. The collection in our house includes two Skeletors, Battle Armor Skeletor, Clawful, Ram Man, Prince Adam and of course He-Man.

Despite their unattractive, even frightening, appearance these figures sure are popular. Apparently, Orko, the magician, is as difficult to find in the stores as a red-haired Cabbage Patch Doll.

Not only preschool boys, but also girls, are enchanted by the show. What's behind the He-Mania? Maybe it's the music, which even I find myself humming.

Or the success might be connected to the faraway setting with the near-to-home moral. At the end of each show, He-Man has a positive message relating the show's story to his viewers' lives.

Maybe the reason is simpler yet. My 4-year-old says he likes it because He-Man is a hero.

Whatever the reason, he's a popular guy. You probably wouldn't want to marry him, but it would be OK if he married your sister.

April 24, 1985

'Supply and Consume' Economist Goes to the 'BIG' Store

Having a big time has found a new definition in my vocabulary.

It used to stand for a night on the town with an elegant candlelight dinner in a fancy restaurant, followed by dancing under the stars and then a walk along the beach watching the sun come up.

Obviously, this kind of big time doesn't occur often, at least not in my life. I think it happens mostly in commercials and soap operas. This new kind of big time is one I had last week.

My friend took me to a warehouse store where everything is big except the prices – that is the reason to go there.

We did it up in a big way. We drove there in my car because it was bigger. I took a big purse with a big wad of money inside. I wore big clothes and we talked big.

I had been eager to go because every time I was at my friend's house we would be eating something big and looking at something bigger that she had bought at this Big store.

She had a box of Grape Nuts so large you needed a forklift to raise it up to pour it into your cereal bowl, a round plastic container of malted milk balls so oversized that when it is empty they plan to use it as a wading pool in the back yard, and a tube of tooth paste that must have been designed for King Kong.

"I've got to see this place," I said, so we went to this land of paper towel by the mile and fingernail polish remover by the bucket. I think the first thing I said upon entering was, "This place is big."

We picked out a big cart to hold all the big stuff we were buying, only to realize we could have used one like the flatbed semi-trailer truck another shopper was hauling behind him.

Our first stop was the office supplies aisle. I was out of computer paper but I won't be again soon. The stock I bought would easily accommodate several printings of "Gone With the Wind."

After each selection I made, I had to say, "Now I won't need to buy that again for awhile."

I was buying all sorts of big things I desperately needed, like the big bag of peanut M & M's. I also picked up some things I didn't exactly need but bought because I was getting carried away with the big savings I was making at the Big store. For example, the bag of big sponges wasn't exactly a high priority. My friend tried to discourage me.

"You only want them because the colors match your house."

"Not true," I said. "I want to clean my house with them. They are so Big."

"Too big," she responded. "You can strap two on your feet, two on your hands and two on your knees and really mop the place up."

"Good idea," I said, and I bought them.

I also bought big stuff that didn't last a long time.

The candy came in big bags and I bought one to have around for weekend company. The kids thought it would be good to have around for that afternoon but not for that evening. They ate it all up by 5 o'clock. OK, I helped them out a bit . . . all right, a lot.

My friend and I had in-depth discussions about the prices. Was it really cheaper to buy things in the extra grand sizes?

We analyzed the jumbo box of detergent. I didn't think it was a better deal than buying several regular boxes at the grocery store but I couldn't decide if I was remembering the right price.

Blueberry muffin mix was another mixing bowl of contention. The Big Store sold three mixes in one, which was several cents less than the regular stores' individual costs. Was the savings worth it?

I said no because at my house we live by the theory of supply and consume. I supply and they consume.

If we had one blueberry muffin mix, they'd make one. If we had three, all three would be opened, made, burned or dumped on the floor.

The bottom line is, did I save money? I don't think so, but you can't expect to in the big time.

July 20, 1988

Road of Life Is Paved with Car Pools

I was driving the car pool to play practice. As we stopped to pick up one of the riders, his sister came outside their house to say she didn't know where he was.

"Do you think he's still at school?" I asked.

"Mom, he's not here. Let's go," Colleen said from the back seat of the car.

"Go ahead, my mom will bring him," the sister yelled. I suggested a few more alternative locations for the brother. After hearing, "I don't know where he is, my mom will bring him," a few more times, followed by a persistent "Let's go, she said he's not here" from Colleen, I drove off

As we left, I began my car pool lecture.

"Do you think that young man's mother will be happy to drive him, when he could have had a ride with us?"

"I don't know. What difference does it make?" Colleen wondered.

"What difference does it make? It makes a lot of difference," I said in a volume-escalating tone. "What if he missed his ride just because he was in the bathroom? No parent likes to drive all over tarnation, taking kids someplace when it's not their turn to drive. The reason parents arrange car pools is so they don't have to drive all the time. You should be more considerate of your parents who are also your chauffeurs."

"I feel a column coming on," said Colleen's friend Michelle, who also was sitting in the back seat.

I figured she was right. So I continued writing out loud as I drove down Center Street.

You are in too many activities in too many places. (Don't I sound like an old fud?) In order to get to most of them, you have to be driven by parents.

Since I'm a parent, I think I'm qualified to say we aren't crazy about doing all this driving.

When you are a passenger in a car pool, remember a few things.

First, be appreciative. Chances are good when a mother picks you up that she already has made several stops and starts in her car.

Her nerves are on edge because another equally frazzled driver with a carload of soccer players or ballet dancers cut in front of her, which made her slam on her brakes, which caused her 2-year-old, who always climbs out of his car seat, to smash against the dashboard.

But she can't stop to console him because, if she did, your car pool would be late.

After you are deposited, she still can't go home, put her feet up and drink a diet cola.

By this time, the Brownies have finished meeting and she has to pick them up, then stop at the grocery store and the cleaners before going back to get your group.

Another thing: Never get upset when your ride is late. The driver is not tardy because she was trying out new lipstick colors at the makeup counter of a discount store.

It's more likely that when the driver was all set to leave the house, she couldn't find her car keys or her kids' shoes or her kids.

Or maybe one of her kids threw a fit because he didn't want to leave in the middle of She-Ra on TV. Or the phone rang, or a diaper suddenly needed changing.

When you get in the car, say something pleasant. A woman who has been driving up and down hills and in and out of driveways, who has been opening and closing car doors and snapping and unsnapping seat belts, and mumbling to herself, "Be patient, practice patience, you'll get through this," isn't sure she wants to make conversation, or even listen to other people making conversation.

Finally, I said to Colleen, who was trying to keep the baby quiet, to Michelle, who had Mike asleep on her lap, and to Molly, who was trying to convince Pete that she wasn't sitting on his seat belt, "Remember to take full advantage of all these dancing lessons, acting classes and team sports, because it is just the training you will need to prepare you for life.

A life like mine, one in the car.

November 19, 1986

Sporting Events Keep Cupboards Stocked

At the time of my wedding, I was busy choosing just the right silver flatware, china and crystal patterns.

I felt it was absolutely necessary to have these things for all the formal occasions I was certain to have.

At the same time, I deliberated thoroughly in choosing what was described as everyday dishes and glassware.

By some miracle, the sets of the "good stuff" are still intact. I think they have lasted because my formal occasions have not occurred as often as I thought they would, thank goodness.

However, my everyday sets are down to memento status, with only the gravy boat left, no milk glasses and only one juice tumbler.

This doesn't affect our lifestyle at all because now our china is by Chinette – the disposable kind – and our crystal is from sporting events.

We are a very lucky family to have glasses galore from every event in town and many from out of town. Each of these 16-ounce or larger plastic cups are decorated with words and pictures of an event.

Our most recent set came from the 1988 College World Series, where our kids spent enough on refreshments to create a new NCAA baseball scholarship. Then they gathered cups left in the bleachers by other sports fans who apparently don't appreciate the finer things.

After all, it is written in blue on the cup that they are No. 2 in a collector series. We had No. 1 from last year's series, but all the ink washed off in the dishwasher.

We have other sets made up of Omaha Royals and Creighton Bluejays cups, and of course, no home in Nebraska would be truly representative of the Cornhusker state without at least one Go Big Red cup.

I surveyed a friend's cupboard and discovered cups touting the escapades of Roger Rabbit, heralding the upcoming Summer Olympics, souvenirs from a visit to the Air Force Academy and a favor from a college fraternity formal.

We use these cups every day, from breakfast to bedtime. They get left in the car, out on the lawn, down in the basement, upstairs in the bedrooms, but we never run short of them. For every plastic cup we misplace, five new ones take its place after a rock concert or an air show.

In addition, there is a lot of swilling of drinks in this watering hole from cups obtained at fast-food and quick-stop shopping places.

Some are refillable for a portion of the original cost, some have tops, and some even have built-in plastic straws. This is the most popular style.

I wonder if its success has anything to do with the similarity to a baby bottle. The teen-ager sipping all day long on his Big Squeeze is operating on the same principle as the toddler who conducts his business of the day with his bottle close by so he can take a swig whenever he gets thirsty.

Some of the other glasses we found were the Big Gusher, which you have to fill up when you have a powerful thirst. You also have to be powerfully strong to hold the cup to your mouth.

If you are slurpy or sloppy, you can slurp some refreshment from a Super Slurpee glass.

The Kum and Go is for folks who aren't sure if they are coming or going, but always want to come in dry and go out wet.

The Border Buster and the Border Cooler are what you drink if you are on the lam and running from the law.

Anyone whose favorite song is Little Brown Jug probably would want to drink from the Little Pop Jug, Movin' Jug Jr. or the Chug-a-jug.

What kind of cup do I like to drink from? I can never decide, so I take it straight from the bottle.

August 10, 1988

Monkee Business Brings Together Mother's, Children's Generations

"OK, OK, I'll write about the Monkees," I told Colleen. After extremely heavy lobbying from Colleen and her friend, Michelle, I decided to tell you all about this fabulous '60s singing group, the Monkees, which is making a comeback.

Although Colleen is the main Monkeemania fan around here, her hysteria has been contagious. Whenever she baby-sits for the little kids, she entertains them by playing a Monkees tape and getting our little monkeys to sing and dance along. Until I told Colleen to quit it, she was answering the phone by saying, "Monkeeland." Now 3-year-old Mike insists on getting on the phone and saying, "Hey, hey, we're the Monkees."

Horan

Colleen also thinks we should name the new baby Davey, so all our little boys will have the same names as the Monkees: Mickey, Mike, Peter and Davey. That is if we change Johnny's name to Mickey.

Recently, the Monkees appeared in concert in Omaha. Lucky for Colleen's dad, Michelle's dad took the girls to see them. When Colleen arrived home flushed with excitement, I politely listened to her account of the evening, and then I started looking through her souvenir program.

"Herman's Hermits were there?" I asked.

"You've heard of them?" Colleen asked.

I turned the page. "Gary Puckett and the Union Gap were there, too? I would love to see them perform."

"You've heard of them, too?" Colleen said in disbelief.

"How could you remember those guys and not care about the Monkees?"

"I remember the Monkees, but I guess I never paid much attention to them."

"Mom, what groups did you like in the '60s?"

"The Beatles and the Supremes were my favorites," I answered.

My friend Phyllis used to come over to our house, stand in front of the fireplace in our family room pretending it was a stage and using a vacuum cleaner hose as microphone would imitate Diana Ross, the leader of the Supremes whenever "Baby Love" came on the radio. It was a great performance.

"How did you dress then?" Colleen asked. "Did you ever wear sleeveless turtlenecks?"

"I think that is what we wore with miniskirts and most of our minidresses were sleeveless."

"Did you save any of them?"

"I only saved things with sentimental memories."

"You mean that old box of junk in the basement? That stuff is only good for dressing up as a nerd. Didn't you save anything that I could wear now?"

"I guess not."

It's too bad that I didn't, but I doubt she'd use the old clothes except to dress up the little kids to impersonate the Monkees.

As you have probably noticed, the music and clothes of the '60s are becoming popular again, but the kids of the '80s are wearing hairstyles from the '50s. In the mid-60s, I thought a flattop, a buzz or a Mohawk were really out-of-it haircuts. Everyone had to have hair, long hair, to be with it.

Since I was born in the late '40s, the number of years I've had to live to get me to the 1980s has worn down my acceptance level. I don't think I could enjoy or even tolerate looking at a nation of long-hairs, especially if some of them lived right in this house. So despite my aversion to the modern-day adaptations of the 1950's crewcut, especially the Mohawk, I can put up with them because at least they are clean and neat-looking.

For the 13 years that I've been a parent, I've been warned that my troubles won't really begin until my children become teen-agers. But I figure if they like the same music I liked as a teen-ager, wear the same style of clothes, and we don't have to argue about the length of their hair, life has to be at least bearable. Well, at least until those white go-go boots surface again.

July 16, 1986

Today's Finds, Tomorrow's Garage Sale Items

When I drove into our driveway, the car loaded up with kids, mine and a few extra, one of my passengers noticed the sign across the street.

"They're having a garage sale at Kevin's house," she said. "Can we go over?" They all begged.

"Sure," I said. I decided to go over too, visit with Kevin's mother and see how the sale was going.

My entourage and I trooped across the street and into our neighbor's garage where we found my neighbor, her visiting relative who was helping out and acting as head cashier, and the typical assortment of garage sale stuff: furniture, clothes, kitchen things, tools, toys and wall decorations.

You would have thought my kids were in Macy's at Christmas, although they have never been there. As a matter of fact, neither have I, but I've heard it's something.

"Can I go home and get my money?" Johnny asked.

"Can I go with him?" Mike asked as he clapped his hands together in excitement.

The girls were going "ga-ga" over the jewelry. "Look at this beautiful necklace," Machaela said. "Can I have a quarter?"

Marie, Machaela's friend, found an equally magnificent piece so I sprang for another quarter, then cousin Erin came up with the real find, an Egyptian-style medallion with blue stones. I thought of arm wrestling her for it.

Maureen, of course, was immediately attracted to the dressy clothes. She had to have a white lacy blouse with puffed sleeves and a black bow tie. It is very pretty and should fit her in five or six years.

By this time the little guys were back with their mad money. Johnny saves the change he finds around the house supposedly to give to the poor, but he delved into it for this sale of sales.

They were finding all sorts of things. On the top bunk of the bunk beds that were for sale were several stuffed animals. The guys were too short to see so I had to lift each of them up to make his selections. We probably have 2 to 3 hundred stuffed animals stuffed all over the house, but Johnny, Mike, and even Pete needed more.

Johnny spread his money, which was in pennies, nickels and dimes and too heavy to hold, on a chair. and everyone helped themselves to it when they discovered a great treasure.

A big hit were the red, white, and blue crepe paper accordion streamers selling for 5 cents. Everyone bought one of those to save for the Fourth of July. (They didn't make it to the holiday; they disintegrated in the rain, making our driveway look very patriotic.)

Other purchases were a puzzle map of the United States, a set of Lego blocks and a puzzle of Huskie dogs. After spending a lot of time and a fair sum of money, I suggested that we go home. I had put off leaving because I figured the longer we were out, the longer the house would stay neat.

When we first got home everyone was content with the new loot. The girls were modeling the jewelry and the boys were building with the blocks, but the lure of a sale across the street was too much to resist.

Soon they were begging to go back. There were things they had to buy, such as the orange brocade pillow, the stuffed lion, the wood tick-tack-toe game, the teething ring and the orange juice glass which Machaela dropped and broke before she got out of the garage.

That evening when John came home from work and saw all the purchases cast about the house, he inquired what had gone on. I told him about the garage sale.

"Well, it looks like it was fun," he said.

"Yes, it was," I said. "And now I'm thinking it might be fun if we had a garage sale and sold it all back."

June 17, 1987

VCR Family Hits Replay Button

Did you miss watching your favorite television show last night?

If so, you probably could watch it at our house. We are living in the VCR (videocassette recorder) age and my kids are recording most of it.

Whenever a show gets taped at our house, it's not only watched, it's memorized. The latest kick is the TV show "Rags to Riches." The kids have every episode on tape, which they replay and replay.

Luckily it is a cute show set in the '60's about five orphan girls taken in by a swinging and rich bachelor. It's sort of a musical, with the girls and the dad singing their versions of popular '60's songs.

On the day after the big snow, the previous evening's episode played continually until everyone, including the painters working on the house, were singing, "I love him, I love him," from one of the show's songs and saying, "I don't want to miss the Untouchables," one of the show's lines.

Another tape, "Better Off Dead," has been run so many times that 2-year-old Pete thinks he's one of the characters. He runs around the house with a head band over his eyes saying, "I want my 2 dollars," a line from the movie (It's better than the name sounds).

When the situation comedy "The Cavanaughs" premiered, I had Patrick tape it because I couldn't watch when it was scheduled. I was interested to see if the TV Cavanaugh family got into as many predicaments as my Cavanaugh family does.

After seeing the show numerous times with the boring scenes fast-forwarded and the good scenes played again and again, I decided it would be great if I could do that with the action around here.

Sometimes on the weekends we rent a move from a video store. Patrick and John usually go out to get it.

I say, "Get something funny," and the under-10 crowd says, "Get something for us."

Seeing what they bring home, I usually think I should have gone along to act as a censor. The movie with a shaky PG-13 rating that I can comfortably watch in a dark movie theatre, I don't want in my family room.

I don't plan on watching the movie until the kids are in bed, but they are never all in bed at once.

Usually Mike falls asleep earlier watching the tape of the Muppett movie and is wide awake, playing with Lego blocks and ready to key in on the television screen just when I wish he wouldn't.

In addition to shows off TV and movies from video stores, we also have quite a collection of tapes made with our video camera by the resident movie maker, Patrick and his buddy, Tom.

I have to admit these movies are clever, even though the boys make a big mess that they promise to clean up after filming but never do.

The latest series involves a dummy you are supposed to think is Patrick because it is dressed like Patrick, who is playing the role of a spy. They film the dummy getting thrown off the roof of our house, and the next scene is one of Patrick landing on the ground.

For the last few years at Christmas they've made their own version of the "Christmas Carol" using our little kids and Tom's younger brother and sister as the cast.

I try to appreciate their creativity when they traipse all over the house and yard rearranging furniture and dragging out clothes for costumes to film the different scenes of Scrooge's Christmas.

The moral to this story is you don't only live once, because once you've been videotaped, you can be freeze-framed, fast-forwarded and rewound over and over.

April 15, 1987

• •

Some Horning In Is Appreciated

I had driven over to pick up Colleen at her friend's house. As I waited for her to collect her things, I visited with the friend's mom. I inquired who else lived in the neighborhood.

"Well, the Honkers live next door." As I looked across the driveway I said, "Oh really. That's not the name on the mailbox."

Just at that moment a car pulled up in front of the Honkers' house and began honking.

"Now do you understand the name?" my friend asked.

"We don't need clocks at our house," she continued. "We schedule our days according to the Honkers' honks. The first sound I hear every morning is at 7 a.m. when Mr. Honker's carpool pulls up to the house and honks. After that initial alarm I have the luxury of turning over and even dropping off to sleep, because at 7:22 I can count on the toot, toot, ta, toot, toot of Junior Honker's lift to prep school to roust me out of bed.

"I try to have myself dressed, the kids up and breakfast started before Honky Honker's 7:45 long, steady blast to hurry up her twin sister, Tonky Honker, who never hears the horn because she's still blow-drying her hair. So Honky blows again at 7:48. Between these two toots I can cook a perfect three-minute egg."

"At 8:15 when Little Honker's preschool ride does a little beep-beep, I usher my family out the door."

"I congratulate myself on a successful morning if I have the beds made and the kitchen straightened up by 9 a.m. when Mama

Honker backs out of the garage and lays on the horn until the family dog, Ho-Hum Honker, finally moves from his resting place on the driveway."

"Gee," I said, "Those people must get on your nerves."

"Oh, not at all. They're great neighbors, even if they will be responsible for making the doorbell obsolete," she went on.

"We've come to depend on their honking. Why, last winter their whole family went on a ski trip. While they were gone, our schedule was completely out of whack. We overslept every morning, my husband spent too much time in the shower, I left my electric curlers in too long and the kids dilly-dallied through their cereal."

By this time Colleen was ready to go. As we were driving home my thoughts started wandering; I was thinking about the Honker family. I didn't notice when the stoplight turned green, but the car behind me did and quickly started honking.

The driver's impatience seemed rather rude. I was tempted to put my car in reverse and back into him to put a silencer on his horn, but I didn't. I had this feeling that if I did, some family wouldn't get their morning wake-up call.

May 26, 1982

10 • TRIPS AND SLIP UPS

You Can't Get There From Here

I just got home from the grocery store. We don't live that far away, but the drive took long enough for my ice cream bars to melt, my hamburger buns to mold and my milk to turn to cottage cheese.

The streets are torn up for repairs. Usually the work just made for slow going, but today it was almost impossible to get home.

After weaving through one-lane traffic where a bridge is being rebuilt, I arrived at the street leading to our neighborhood. It was barricaded.

I thought about driving around the barricade, but decided the work crews down the street wouldn't be very happy if I put tire tracks on the new surface.

If I were to drive a little farther . . . then weave my way back through a nearby neighborhood, I would end up at the bottom of my hill.

All I would need to do is cross the street being surfaced, drive up the hill and into my driveway!

When I reached this point, it was also barricaded. I would have driven around the barricade, but trucks were parked on either side.

I thought about getting out of the car and moving the barricade. Once again the presence of workmen on the road discouraged my boldness.

Instead I sat in the car to consider my options, and figured I didn't have many. I backed down the street, turned around and began driving.

When I passed the home of a friend – one I used to think lived really close to me – she was outside getting the mail, so I stopped.

"I'm trying to get home, but I can't figure out how to do it," I said.

"You have a problem," Esther said. "Maybe you could try going down and turning by the nursery."

This wasn't a possibility that appealed to me. It meant going back to the road with the bridge out and the section of one-lane traffic.

Now that the rush hour was creeping closer, the cars were creeping along. Eventually, someone let me into the traffic and we crept along together. I was patient because my turn was not far away.

Once again, my routing plans went awry. A "no left turn" sign and an approaching police car put turning out of the question.

I drove until I could turn around in the parking lot of a muffler shop. I drove back to make a legal turn. Once I did this, getting home was finally an achievable goal.

I don't want to complain. I should be grateful that I have a car and that I live in an area where road maintenance is important. I can't help but be frustrated by the annual summer road work.

One advantage of living in this part of the country is that we don't have the traffic congestion found in larger cities. Yet our opportunities to enjoy this advantage seem few.

When travel around town isn't slowed by widening and resurfacing, it's slowed by the peril of winter ice and snow.

After a long winter of sliding into stop signs and cars and sometimes off the road, everyone is happy to see spring arrive, even if it means the beginning of street construction and repair.

But tempers seem to heat up with summer temperatures, as we cool our heels in a hot car that is not moving.

The solution? Getting a helicopter is an idea. I wonder if any grocery store has a helipad?

July 23, 1986

Cavanaughs Go to Washington

As I put my head down on the pillow, a joint sigh of relief was heard in the bedroom.

"Well, we made it there and back," I said.

"It's pretty amazing, isn't it?" John answered.

We had just returned from taking our seven children plus Patrick's friend, Tommy, on a five-day trip to Washington, D.C., for my sister's wedding.

I've been told that I'm an Occasion Person, someone who makes every occasion an Occasion. Certainly a family wedding qualified as an occasion to make an Occasion.

Horan

My expectations for this trip were very high. I had planned and plotted each detail for over a month. I wanted the trip to be fun, educational, and most of all memorable. I wanted things to run smoothly.

Every day for weeks before, I had conversations with Johnny and Mike about their behavior, particularly in church, so they wouldn't spoil Mary Pat's wedding. Crabbing and hanging onto Mom were not allowed.

I had a picture in my mind of how everyone should dress for every event. I even wrote a list of who would wear what when.

You're right. Things didn't go quite as I had planned.

But all in all, things went as smoothly as you could expect for two adults who spent the whole trip counting to nine. (Our original eight companions were increased to nine on the second day, when Omaha cousin Molly joined our entourage.)

The event the children most likely will remember is the aroma of the plane trip, when air sickness became a popular in-flight pastime.

On the takeoff, Peter, the baby, had a takeoff of his own, which landed all over me. Colleen performed on both takeoff and landing, but she managed to hit the air sickness receptacle provided by the airlines.

Patrick wasn't so lucky. Or maybe I should say 2-year-old Mike wasn't.

As we began our descent into Washington, Patrick, who was holding Mike, plopped down in an empty seat to have a better view of the monuments.

The nice gentleman in the adjoining seat engaged Patrick in a conversation.

"Do you plan on seeing all the sights while you are in Washington?"

"Yes," Patrick said. "I just hope I feel better when I get there."

"Oh, I hope you do, too. There's so much to see."

Patrick agreed, and then immediately deposited his in-flight snack all over himself and Mike, creating a crown effect on Mike's hair.

Mike probably felt like a guy who was in the wrong place at the wrong time, but he maintained his composure. He promptly fell asleep after the steward gingerly set him back in his seat for the landing.

Maureen especially will remember everyone getting back to the hotel from sightseeing a mere 40 minutes before it was time to leave for the wedding.

After a rapid round of baths, shampoos and hair-drying, we discovered that Maureen had gum stuck on both of her ears and in her hair.

After unsuccessfully trying to comb it out, I tried pulling it out. That resulted in a hunk of hair in my hand, a lot of tears on Maureen's face, and a wad of gum still in her hair.

I sent Colleen off to get scissors from one of my sisters who was also staying in the hotel. She came back with nail clippers, which worked just as well.

After that crisis, I was hurriedly attempting to curl Maureen's hair when I burned her forehead with the curling iron. At that point, I decided that gum looked just fine on her.

Many scenes will always stand out in my memory: Mary Pat entering the church, looking radiant and beautiful in the dress my mother wore 41 years before; all my three brothers and four sisters at the reception taking turns dancing with their spouses, their children and each other; my mom and dad dancing together at the end of the reception; the thrill Machaela felt at the Smithsonian Institution when she saw the ruby shoes Dorothy wore in "The Wizard of Oz"; my family standing at the Jefferson Memorial while John read and explained Thomas Jefferson's words on freedom and liberty inscribed on the marble.

I've been wanting to buy new dining room chairs for a long time. Maybe if we hadn't taken this trip I could have purchased them.

But instead of chairs, I have all my memories. I know I can't sit on memories, but I can hold them in my heart. And if throughout their lives my children feel a tiny tinge of joy each time our visit to Washington is reminisced, it will have been worthwhile.

May 22, 1985

Kitty with the Urge to Roam Is as Much Trouble as a Child

I have seven children and a cat.

If you were to whistle over my responsibilities, it probably would be over my number of offspring. It certainly wouldn't be because of my cat. Cats are supposed to be easy to care for, unlike children, husbands or even dogs. And most cats are, except ours.

He's got ants in his pants, the urge to roam or miles to go before he sleeps. His gallivanting never created a problem until recently, when our kitty got into the car of a guest who was leaving my across-the street neighbor's bridge party.

Horan

Luckily, Maureen saw the kitty staring out the car window as the lady drove away. She ran into the house to report this news to her Dad and Grandma. As they were deciding what to do, Maureen ran upstairs and came down holding her rosary beads and a picture of Augie – that's the kitty's name.

Grandma tried to console her by saying, "Don't worry, Maureen, cats always find the way home again," to which Maureen responded between sobs, "But Grandma, he can't even read our address."

In the meantime our neighbor, Jean, had called the guest, who had arrived home, discovered her extra passenger and let him out of the car. She thought he was the neighbor's cat and had ridden to the party with her.

Maureen and John drove over to the lady's home with plans to search her neighborhood, but they found the kitty right away, in her garage on top of the garbage cans.

One Sunday, the kitty was playing in the front yard. A short time later he was gone. At first, I wasn't concerned. He had run off before and made it back to the house. But when it got dark, I started worrying a bit. The kitty didn't come back all night.

In the morning I called the Humane Society, two radio stations that report lost pets and the vet's office and asked my neighbors to watch for him. Then I drove around to look for him, but had no luck.

By 3 o'clock I was feeling pretty low. I dreaded the scene when the kids came home from school and learned the kitty was still missing. I wondered what had happened to him. Did he get hit by a car? Did a big cat or dog get him? Where did he sleep last night? Did he get cold?

Then the phone rang. A lady on the line said she had gotten our number from the Humane Society.

"Do you have my cat?" I asked.

"Well, if he's less than a year old and is orange with a white chest, I do. Last night I discovered him in our garage, and when he was still there this morning, I figured he was lost."

After I brought Augie home, I called the vet's office. We had decided it was time to surgically take care of his wander-lust tendencies before he wandered in front of a speeding car.

Augie must have known what was in store, because he disappeared again the next day, despite my attempts to keep track of him. That evening Patrick and I searched all around the neighborhood, without success. Later that night, our doorbell rang. Kelly, our neighbor's daughter from two blocks away, stood at the door holding Augie. She had found him in a garage. I wasn't surprised.

I later told a friend that the kitty was as much trouble as another child. He replied, "True, but the difference between the two is you have to keep the kids, but you could get rid of the cat."

That's the problem. I can't get rid of the kitty because I like him and I would miss him. Even if he needs to go on an adventure a day, I know that in his heart he feels, "There's no place like home," if he can only find it.

Now that he wears a collar and tag with his name and address, maybe he will have better luck.

March 26, 1986

Few Medals Given in Parent Marathon

We have a friend who is building himself up to compete in the Ironman triathlon. This event consists of running a long way, riding a bike an even longer way, and then swimming a couple miles in the ocean.

He has tried to convince John and me that this is something we should do. I expressed doubt at my ability to do this. I know I don't have the desire to do it, but my friend insists I would like it if I were to start training.

Lucky for me I won't have to consider it, because John and I have already done the Ironman. We just returned from taking our eight children on a Colorado ski trip.

I'd be surprised if a triathlon required more mental endurance and physical stamina than our trip. We had a great time, at least that is what I kept telling myself while I was there, and it was an adventure, at least that's how I've described the trip since we returned home.

The buildup for this trip lasted seven years.

Each year since late 1980 we have traveled to Colorado for a ski trip with our friends from Denver, Kam and Mike Martin and their children. The first year, John and our oldest two children went.

I stayed home because Johnny was a baby. The next year I went along because it was what the Martins started calling a non-pregnant year.

The next year I didn't go. John took the oldest two children, plus Maureen, right after Mike's birth.

We have pretty much followed this pattern. Each year that we added a skier to the party – they had to be at least kindergarten age – we also would add a baby to the family. This was the year to add Johnny and also the year of Matthew's arrival.

I suggested that I stay home with the three little guys, but the Martins and John thought otherwise. They said, "It won't be any fun without you." I could understand that logic since am I so much fun. So we all went.

The three parts of our Ironman – or Ironwoman – included the trip out (we drove), the time spent at the mountain and the trip back. It rained and snowed all the way and I left my purse with John's wallet inside it in a Bonanza restaurant in York, NE.

"You know this sport has to be a lot of fun to make us go to this much trouble to get organized," Mike Martin said to John as they equipped the young skiers.

Several times during the trip we discussed what we should do, or what we should have done. Most of our "should" conversations revolved around money.

Since the cost of skiing can escalate in a hurry, I was interested in deals and coupons. I made John stop at a Vickers gas station in Denver to buy a coupon book with discounts for ski school and lift tickets. We only bought one book. We should have bought several. We also should have purchased our under-12 lift tickets there because they were cheaper than at the resort. Next year we will!

Getting everyone dressed in long underwear, ski socks, turtleneck sweaters, ski jackets and pants, hats, mitten liners and mittens, finding the sunglasses or goggles, putting on the sunblock, putting on the ski boots and then hauling the little ones who can't walk in the ski boots, and carrying their skis and poles plus our own to the chairlift lines is the ultimate test of inner, outer and any other kind of strength you can think of.

I didn't ski much because I didn't want to leave the little ones, Pete and Matt, in a nursery. What if they cried? John finally convinced me that I should and Pete did cry – but he got over it. He says now he loved the Belly Button Bakery, the resort's day-care center, but he doesn't want to go back because they make you take a nap.

Mike and Johnny went to ski school. Johnny did great and Mike said he liked skiing except he couldn't stop.

Patrick, Colleen, Maureen, Machaela and the Martin kids won medals in NASTAR, a timed downhill ski race.

John and I didn't enter. We're holding out for that big medal you get in the sky. After this trip we surely qualify.

April 8, 1987

• •

Counting the Miles on Road to Vacation

It is 319.1 miles from my driveway to the Mississippi River. From the Mississippi to Interstate 51 which is now numbered Interstate 39 where we turn north from the former Illinois 5 which is now Illinois tollway 88, it is 84.1 miles. From that point until our destination, Lake Geneva, WI, it is 70.8 miles.

Fascinating? Not really. Not now anyway, but it was en route to the lake the other day. So fascinating in fact it consumed the eight hours and one minute of our time in the car. When we left home I wrote down the mileage registered on the car's odometer and the time. We forgot to note the mileage after one hour but by the two-hour mark we all eagerly watched the clock so we could get a precise mileage.

I wrote it down and subtracted to find out how far we had traveled in two hours. After that we talked about other things, I don't remember what, and fiddled with the car's tape deck. We had a Billy Joel tape I wanted to hear but we couldn't get the tape deck out of the rewind gear. Eventually, the third hour rolled up on the clock. When we figured we had traveled almost 40 percent of the way, everyone cheered.

We started discussing lunch and when we would stop to eat it. In anticipation of that occasion, the high point of our trip, we broke out a bag of animal cookies and passed them around.

At our lunch and gas stop, despite my warnings that we wouldn't be stopping again, whole cans of pop were popped open around the gas station picnic table which wasn't a picnic table at all but a cement slab underneath the Sinclair sign. Not a picturesque locale but we had our agenda. Therefore, there was no time to scout for scenic beauty.

Back on the road after lunch, we began serious calculations. We began figuring out the mileage (on the hour from our luncheon departure time we proceeded to figure the hourly mileage from our morning departure time). Then we moved on to calculating our arrival time by figuring out the miles per hour we had traveled since lunch and dividing that into the number of miles left to our destination.

"If my calculations, are correct," (I said to myself they ought to be after all the figuring), "we should be at the lake in time for Saturday evening Mass." This idea was quickly seconded by my car mates who liked visualizing the next morning, the beginning of their first day at the lake, not interrupted with dressing up and trekking to church. Being the mother, I suggested we think of the church stop as a time of thanksgiving for a safe journey instead of an obligation, but as a potential beach bum I was quietly doing somersaults of glee.

After we decided to stop off at church before pulling up to the lake house we still had a problem. We were traveling in tandem with another car. In my car were myself, my five sons, and my college niece, Kathy, who did all the driving so I could do all the refereeing. In the other car were my three girls and a college-age friend, Colleen, who was driving. John, the husband and Dad, missed the big sojourn and was to join us for the second half of our vacation and the flip-flop of our drive.

Since stopping was not allowed on the itinerary we had to signal our church plans to the car behind. We did this by hanging a note on the toll booth coin basket addressed to the Colleens in the car behind us.

Finally we arrived! The total trip 475 miles. I knew you'd want to know that.

August 17, 1988

• •

Siblings, Offspring Equal a Houseful

I was in charge of counting beds, which meant first I had to count the heads which would go into the beds.

The number of beds remained constant but the number of heads changed daily.

My family, which consists of myself, husband and eight children, was gathered at my parents' summer place in Fontana on Geneva Lake, WI, with all the members of my extended family, which includes my parents, my three brothers, four sisters, their spouses and children.

You'll probably be relieved, as my parents were, that none of my siblings has produced as many offspring as I have.

Nevertheless, it was a houseful. The house that always had extra space when I was merely one of eight was bulging to the rafters now that I am also the mother of eight.

As you can imagine, this bed-and-head counting was a tough job, but my able assistant Barbara – my New Jersey sister – and I accepted the challenge of heading up the family's bedding down.

My mother wanted to get into the act, but we nixed the idea and instructed her to concentrate on praying for good weather and no bugs so we could eat outside.

Early on, Barbara and I realized there were several more heads than beds. The attic ordinarily sleeps 14 but for this assemblage we decided to stretch it to 17.

The "hen house," which is my dad's name for the attic because in the summers of old it housed his five daughters and our continual influx of girlfriends, can no longer be just for hens because all of his hens have mated and now have little chicks, mostly male.

Our first executive decision was for an integrated attic.

Our second edict was, "You sleep where we tell you and be happy about it." This meant everyone had to be nice to Barbara and me in hopes of alighting for the night in a comfortable spot, as opposed to the two lawn cushions pushed together, or on a leaky air mattress.

If you were lucky you could be assigned to what we refer to as the honeymoon suite. It comes complete with a baby crib. The porch swing was another coveted spot, as was the porch floor. I didn't strong-arm anyone to take either of those perches.

No one was exempt from these rulings except Grandma and Grandpa Barrett. Everyone had to be nice to them since it is their house and we all want to be invited back next year.

Plus, their bedroom is the only one exempt from our manipulation. We never once considered putting their mattress on the floor and having three kids sleep on the box springs.

Once we had the sleeping arranged, next on the agenda was the inevitable family picture. All the brothers and sisters had not been together since the last family wedding, so my mother was almost as determined about getting a new picture as she was about us not leaving our "stuff" all over the place, junking things up. Believe me, that is determination.

Just because we were all together at Lake Geneva didn't mean we were ever all assembled at the lakefront where the picture was to be taken. The picture's subjects were either swimming in, sailing on, flying over in my brothers' small plane, or snoozing on the raft in the lake. The sleepers were usually the ones with the crummy bed assignments.

Finally, the photo-opportunity order was issued and all complied. We knew our evening meal depended on being there and smiling prettily.

The resulting snapshot is a portrait of a very relaxed group in swimming suits, shorts and bare feet who were glad to be together.

August 24, 1988

Storm Follows Blizzard of Warnings

My parents asked us not to go, the weather forecaster warned against it, and the travel advisers didn't advise it, but "What the heck," we thought. "Let's try it."

John and our seven children drove to St. Charles, IL, where I grew up, to spend Thanksgiving with my parents and several of my sisters and brothers.

We had a great time. Sunday came too soon, but when it arrived it was time to start the 450 mile drive back to Omaha.

The Iowa forecast for blizzardlike conditions wasn't encouraging, but we needed to get going. The older kids had school on Monday, John had to go to work and I had laundry. So we set out.

Despite the heavy rain that was falling in northern Illinois, we were able to move along until we crossed the Mississippi River. The weather changed dramatically for the worse. Patrick said, "If these are blizzardlike conditions, I sure hope we don't run into blizzard conditions."

Cars were sliding off the interstate, some were spinning around in front of us, and trucks were overturning. After 10 minutes of watching these adventures and praying that we would not become participants in them, I said, "Let's stop." John agreed.

We could barely see a small hotel off in the distance. We drove to it. The parking lot was jammed with cars and trucks.

John went inside to see if we could get a room. He was gone for 45 minutes, but it seemed longer.

I spent the time counting the number of windows in the motel and trying to count the number of cars in the parking lot to determine if there would be enough rooms to go around. It wasn't a very scientific survey because the windshield was nearly iced over.

When John finally emerged holding keys to the motel's last double rooms, I was so grateful. I'd had visions of bedding everyone down in a gas station between the tire display and the windshield wiper refills.

After we got situated, John and Patrick went to the gas station to get some food – the motel didn't have a restaurant. They returned with a junk food junkie's dream: potato chips, corn chips, popcorn, candy bars and cans of pop.

As the day dragged on, more stranded folks stopped at the motel. Unfortunately, they weren't able to get rooms.

As the hall began filling up, Maureen and Machaela acted like Red Cross volunteers. They gave the weary travelers the chairs from our room, they passed out popcorn and offered soft drinks. They invited people into our room to watch television and use the bathroom.

I encouraged this hospitality and even made my own disaster relief overtures. I felt a twinge of guilt that I had a place to sleep and they didn't.

On Monday morning, it didn't take us long to get ready to go. Everyone had slept dressed. The lock on our cartop carrier was frozen shut so we had to get along without our pajamas and toothbrushes.

When we set out the wind had died down, the sky was blue and the interstate had just been reopened for travel, but the roads were still slick.

We drove the first 60 miles in three hours. I spent the whole time telling John how to drive, saying Hail Marys and holding onto Colleen, who was sitting next to me.

How did our children act? They were remarkably good, especially the two youngest, Mike and Peter, who slept most of the time. At one point, Johnny started complaining about the location of his seat.

Patrick told him, "Don't crab, you might make Dad go off the road. See that car in the ditch? It probably had a crab riding in it."

During the rest of the trip, every time Johnny saw a car off the road he'd say, "They must have been really crabby."

When we finally arrived home Monday night from our Thanksgiving trip, we all agreed we had something new to be thankful for.

Do we have any Christmas travel plans? No. The farthest we plan to venture is out to the front yard to see if Santa's sleigh is flying over head.

December 18, 1985

Travelers Take in Sights, Seafood

We just finished our airport gift shopping. I bought lobsters and clams, and now we are en route home.

I took Patrick and Colleen, our two biggest kids, and cousin Molly to Boston for the weekend on some bonus airline tickets we had to use up before the end of the year.

It has been a really wonderful time. We stayed at a fancy old hotel at a very reasonable rate, thanks to my sister, the travel agent. I always enjoy myself much more when I'm getting a bargain.

Right now I have all my traveling companions writing down their thoughts about the trip. Colleen has to report to her class. Molly wants to read her book, but I won't let her until she writes. Patrick is willing because I let him make a phone call to his friend on one of the plane's inflight phones and charge it to my credit card.

There were many adventures over the weekend. We took the "T," Boston's subway system, most everywhere we went. It was remarkably fast and very convenient. The only hitch was on the way to the John F. Kennedy Library.

Jim – Molly's dad and my husband's brother, who is temporarily living in Boston to do some legal research – got off the subway first to make sure it was the right stop. Just as he motioned for us to get off, the train doors closed and away we went. It was a perfect chance for me to sing the Kingston Trio song about Charlie who rode forever beneath the streets of Boston on the MTA: "Oh, he never returned . . . ."

Once we were reunited, we made it to the JFK library, where we watched a movie about Kennedy's campaign for the presidency and highlights, disappointments, crises and accomplishments of his time as president. Then we toured the library and viewed the collection of memorabilia.

Kennedy's presidency made a lasting impression on me at a time when I was about the same age as Patrick, Colleen and Molly. The issues that confronted President Kennedy – civil rights in America, human rights in Berlin, protection from radioactive fallout and communism in Cuba – are still being played out in today's world, although the situations and locations are different.

For Patrick, Colleen and Molly, hearing President Kennedy's speeches was a lesson from history that I hope they can apply to their lives to help them make a commitment to improve the world.

Of course, our trip was not all historical stuff. We also made the required trip to Filene's basement, as well as to most every "cool" store in Boston, but our purchases were mostly sweatshirts at Harvard.

We also saw a fun play called "Sheboppin," a '60s rock 'n' roll show. Everyone in our entourage decided my 11-year-old dancing and wiggling daughter, Maureen, would be perfect as one of the lead characters in the show.

Eating – especially seafood – rated high on our list of activities. Since we were walking so much, we figured we could eat twice as much. My favorite restaurant was Legal Seafood, which Colleen kept calling "that legal fish place."

Everyone ordered some sort of seafood, except Molly, who ordered vanilla ice cream because fish is gross. She asked for a bib like the one Patrick wore to eat his lobster.

She did relent in her fish eating abstinence by trying some of my scallops and was amazed when she liked the taste. Patrick ordered shaved ice to put in his milk. They didn't have it.

At The Tasty, a corner luncheonette near Harvard University, I temporarily diverted from my seafood bender to have a cheeseburger, french fries and a frappe (Boston's name for milkshake), served up by a short-order cook who was as fast with the glib lines as he was at slinging hash.

The girls thought he looked like Patrick Swayze, the actor.

On our last day we drove from Boston to Cape Cod. Although the day was cold, we decided it would be fun to see the area, and it was picturesque. We thought it would be nice to see some friends living there and to try the area's seafood again.

Now that we are in Nebraska, it's good to be home.

As a footnote to United Airlines, which I good-naturedly slandered after my last trip, it is only fair to say that this trip was perfect from start to finish, and the new terminal in Chicago is beautiful.

December 9, 1987

11 • LESSONS LEARNED

Friends of Parents' Age 'Accept Us as We Are'

The luncheon was at a favorite spot, a quaint restaurant in a park along the Fox River. I remembered being there for many happy occasions and this was another one, a bridal shower for my sister, Mary Pat.

I got to the table a few minutes late; my mother had sent me home for the forgotten camera. After kisses and hugs were exchanged, I sat down between two sisters, Margie and Mary Johnson.

As I looked out at ducks braving the cold water, the park pavilion in the distance caught my eye. Memories of another happy time, of two young families having a picnic, rushed into my view. "Remember when we came here for the picnic?" I asked.

"Yes," mother answered. "Bert (Margie and Mary's dad) had Wednesday afternoons off and your dad was home, so we brought all of you here."

"Your mom brought along a huge cooler full of pop, and we could have as much as we wanted," I said to Margie and Mary.

"Mom thought at picnics kids should be able to overdo," Margie added.

No one said it, but after this exchange we all felt that one seat was very empty at the table, Margie and Mary's mother, Anne Johnson, was missing. She had died the previous summer. Her family always had taken part in the special occasions of our family, just as we always were in the special times for them.

The luncheon happened several months ago, but I thought about it yesterday when mother called to tell me about the death of another friend's mother, Joyce. What's making me feel so sad, beyond the sadness I feel at losing these two women so soon? I decided my mother isn't the only one who has lost two friends.

I have always thought of Anne as my mother's friend, and of Joyce as my friend's mother. Now I understand that the affection these generations ahead have for their friends' children, and their children's friends, is genuine. It's not demanding, jealous or phony, and it doesn't waver as the course of life takes us in different directions. They have known us all our lives, and they accept us as we are.

I was special to Joyce and Anne. They were interested in me and the things I was doing, even when I was a silly little girl and an even sillier teenager.

The Sorensens lived across the street. Their daughter, Catherine, and I were pals. Mrs. Sorensen (I never could call her Joyce) sewed, and let us use the scraps to make doll clothes. When I was about 9 years old they moved to California. I never really felt they were away, because they returned to Illinois in the summers to visit their grandparents and, of course, us.

And one time I visited them. Everything was done to make sure I had a good time. We went to Disneyland, the beach and a television studio. It was an exciting trip.

The Johnsons were our neighbors at the lake. When Mr. Johnson converted to Catholicism, he asked my mom and dad to be his godparents. When my youngest brother was born, Mr. and Mrs. Johnson were his godparents. All our special times – birthdays, confirmations, graduations, anniversaries and weddings – were intertwined.

It's hard to fill such an empty spot in my heart with memories, but there are so many they can't help but brighten a dark place. I just wish we were still making memories.

November 6, 1985

'How Lucky to Have Such Friends'

Mr. and Mrs. Shodeen are wonderful and dear friends. They are neighbors at Lake Geneva, WI, where my family goes in the summer.

Every winter the Shodeens travel to a warmer climate. Every summer, I invite them to stop off and see us en route.

When they called to say they were coming for a visit, I wasn't home. Later I asked my mother, "John has extra tickets to the Nebraska game. Do you think the Shodeens would be interested in going to it?"

"Well, they'll do just about anything. I think they might really enjoy it," she answered.

She was right. They thought a college football game sounded like a lot of fun. On the morning of the game, Mr. and Mrs. Shodeen arrived at our house outfitted in Husker Red.

After spending some time looking around our place, playing with the children and visiting with me while I packed a Go Big Red lunch, they set out with John, Patrick and friends for Lincoln, where they had such a good time that John said, "The Shodeens became instant alumni."

That evening without even a breather, we commenced socializing and eventually sat down to a delicious meal, cooked by me, topped off with after-dinner games with the kids and a viewing of the World Series.

These good friends have been parents three times, grandparents about 11 times, and great-grandparents at least three times, and they have known me almost all of my life. The difference in our ages is barely noticeable, however.

It is sometimes difficult to decide which of us is older. I like to think that John and I do things, but we're stick-in-the-muds by comparison.

When you know someone for a long time, there usually are happy stories to tell.

We kids always washed our hair in the lake. Once in a while we'd talk the adults into doing it, too, so we could play beauty parlor.

Mrs. Shodeen was always game for this. One time she washed her hair and then sat on the pier while I put curlers in it.

It took me such a long time to finish that I thought her hair was getting too dry and wouldn't curl.

So I got a pail of lake water and threw it at her. I think she was pretty surprised, but all she said was, "This is one benefit they don't offer at my other beauty parlor."

When Donna, the Shodeen's daughter and my good friend, and I were in college we used to go out together on summer evenings. One time when we were on a rather wild streak, Mrs. Shodeen suggested that we come home early that evening instead of "carousing" past midnight.

Mr. Shodeen, who overheard this conversation, wondered aloud what this carousing was about. Mr. Shodeen has a very gentle and observant sense of humor.

When my sister, Mary Pat, asked us how the Shodeens' visit was, John said, "They are really amazing. Bill is such a gentleman with Lill." John can call them by their first names because he hasn't known them all his life.

"Mr. Shodeen is always a gentleman," Mary Pat said. "That must be why marriage has worked for them for over 50 years."

Life is meant to be enjoyed, is the attitude Mr. and Mrs. Shodeen have.

A cynical person might say they are just lucky: They have each other, they are healthy, and they have the resources to enjoy a pleasant lifestyle. Anybody would be happy with these conditions.

This may be true, but some folks are unhappy and no fun to be around no matter what the situation, and others are upbeat and a source of delight under the most adverse conditions.

I prefer the latter kind of person. That's why I think I'm the one with the luck, because I know the Shodeens and even better, I'm inspired by them.

November 12, 1986

Reunion 'War Stories' Include Vietnam

It was late at night. Colleen and I were on a walk around the neighborhood, pushing the baby in the stroller and hoping he would fall asleep, when my 13-year-old daughter asked me, "If you had a choice would you rather have grown up in the '60s or the '80s?"

Since Colleen is always asking "what if?" questions, I was tempted to give her a flip response, but I couldn't think of one. Instead I said, "I'm happy I grew up in the '60s – I had a lot of fun – but there are so many more opportunities for girls now, especially in sports."

"And in the '60s we had Vietnam to contend with. It dominated our lives and the prospects for our future."

"Vietnam seemed far away, yet close to home. When I was in high school I would go over to my friend Phyliss' house. On her parents' kitchen table was a map of Southeast Asia covered with marking pins. It served as a constant reminder that their Marine son was precariously traipsing around too far from home and a safe life.

Years later, copies of that map were still being used in homes all over America. One was even in Grandma and Grandpa's house, keeping track of Uncle Peter's tour of duty."

Recently, when I went with John to Denver for his 20-year college reunion, I took a trip back to those tumultuous days of the miniskirt. We had a wonderful time celebrating with the fellas (it was an all-male school then) and their wives.

There were lots of catching-up conversations about families, jobs, children and hobbies, but the great stories were the ones reliving their four years together. One person compared the warm feeling of camaraderie with that of visiting favorite relatives.

After two days of laughing very hard at stories about the laundry where the clothes always turned pink, the cafeteria where the food was always the same – awful – and roommates who were weird and teachers who were weirder, it occurred to me that everyone there was also telling an army story, because in the late '60s, when school was out, Uncle Sam called you in.

For the most part these military tales were also on the light, even humorous, side. Especially the one about the new recruit telling the quartermaster sergeant, "This size 28 T-shirt you issued me will be way too small."

"Is that a fact?" the sergeant answered. "Then these pants should even out that problem," he said as he handed the recruit a size 44 waist.

The tone was more sober when the remembrances were of someone who didn't make it to the reunion because he never made it back physically or mentally from his post-graduate stint in the jungles, or when those who had visited the Vietnam Memorial in Washington, D.C., described its impact.

One former soldier said it reminded him of a big black scar carved amid the beautiful white symbols of freedom (the Washington Monument and the Jefferson and Lincoln Memorials) which surround it. Someone else described the Vietnam Memorial as a painful reminder of a very tragic time but said it helped to see his friends honored there.

The feelings we experienced at the reunion were so rich and full they have to be shared. Some of the moments, as good as they were, probably would lose something in the retelling. You had to be there. But the opportunity to be with these friends and, after 20 years, to recapture that unique kinship, is one I want my children to have.

What I'm trying to say is that growing up in the '60s turned out to be a good experience for me, one I want my children to have, with one exception: I don't want them to have a Vietnam to talk about at their reunion.

July 29, 1987